Online Resources

Congratulations! You now have access to additional resources on the Consumer Behavior concepts that you will learn in this book. These resources will help you implement your learnings in the real world and give you an in-depth understanding of the concepts.

The templates include:

- Reference videos to enhance understanding of the concepts discussed in the book
- Practical exercises to provide a hands-on approach to learning
- A list of additional tools available for marketers to study consumer behavior
- Additional examples from the real world

I0028031

To access the templates, follow the steps below:

1. Scan this QR code to land on the product page.
2. Request the online resources by filling in the required details.

bit.ly/cb-slm

Happy self-learning!

This page is intentionally left blank

SELF–LEARNING MANAGEMENT SERIES

VIBRANT
PUBLISHERS

CONSUMER BEHAVIOR ESSENTIALS

YOU ALWAYS WANTED TO KNOW

Understanding consumer tribes,
marketing practices, and more

PABLO IBARRECHE

CONSUMER BEHAVIOR ESSENTIALS YOU ALWAYS WANTED TO KNOW

First Edition

Paperback ISBN 10: 1-63651-326-3
Paperback ISBN 13: 978-1-63651-326-3

Ebook ISBN 10: 1-63651-327-1
Ebook ISBN 13: 978-1-63651-327-0

Hardback ISBN 10: 1-63651-328-X
Hardback ISBN 13: 978-1-63651-328-7

Library of Congress Control Number: 2024948967

Vibrant Publishers' books are available at special quantity discount for sales promotions, or for use in corporate training programs. For more information please write to bulkorders@vibrantpublishers.com

Please email feedback / corrections (technical, grammatical or spelling) to spellerrors@vibrantpublishers.com

To access the complete catalogue of Vibrant Publishers, visit www.vibrantpublishers.com

SELF-LEARNING MANAGEMENT SERIES

TITLE	PAPERBACK* ISBN
BUSINESS AND ENTREPRENEURSHIP	
BUSINESS COMMUNICATION ESSENTIALS	9781636511634
BUSINESS ETHICS ESSENTIALS	9781636513324
BUSINESS LAW ESSENTIALS	9781636511702
BUSINESS PLAN ESSENTIALS	9781636511214
BUSINESS STRATEGY ESSENTIALS	9781949395778
ENTREPRENEURSHIP ESSENTIALS	9781636511603
INTERNATIONAL BUSINESS ESSENTIALS	9781636513294
PRINCIPLES OF MANAGEMENT ESSENTIALS	9781636511542

TITLE	PAPERBACK ISBN
COMPUTER SCIENCE AND TECHNOLOGY	
BLOCKCHAIN ESSENTIALS	9781636513003
MACHINE LEARNING ESSENTIALS	9781636513775
PYTHON ESSENTIALS	9781636512938

TITLE	PAPERBACK ISBN
DATA SCIENCE FOR BUSINESS	
BUSINESS INTELLIGENCE ESSENTIALS	9781636513362
DATA ANALYTICS ESSENTIALS	9781636511184

TITLE	PAPERBACK ISBN
FINANCIAL LITERACY AND ECONOMICS	
COST ACCOUNTING & MANAGEMENT ESSENTIALS	9781636511030
FINANCIAL ACCOUNTING ESSENTIALS	9781636510972
FINANCIAL MANAGEMENT ESSENTIALS	9781636511009
MACROECONOMICS ESSENTIALS	9781636511818
MICROECONOMICS ESSENTIALS	9781636511153
PERSONAL FINANCE ESSENTIALS	9781636511849

*Also available in Hardback & Ebook formats

SELF-LEARNING MANAGEMENT SERIES

TITLE	PAPERBACK* ISBN

HR, DIVERSITY, AND ORGANIZATIONAL SUCCESS

DIVERSITY, EQUITY, AND INCLUSION ESSENTIALS	9781636512976
DIVERSITY IN THE WORKPLACE ESSENTIALS	9781636511122
HR ANALYTICS ESSENTIALS	9781636510347
HUMAN RESOURCE MANAGEMENT ESSENTIALS	9781949395839
ORGANIZATIONAL BEHAVIOR ESSENTIALS	9781636512303
ORGANIZATIONAL DEVELOPMENT ESSENTIALS	9781636511481

LEADERSHIP AND PERSONAL DEVELOPMENT

DECISION MAKING ESSENTIALS	9781636510026
INDIA'S ROAD TO TRANSFORMATION: WHY LEADERSHIP MATTERS	9781636512273
LEADERSHIP ESSENTIALS	9781636510316
TIME MANAGEMENT ESSENTIALS	9781636511665

MODERN MARKETING AND SALES

CONSUMER BEHAVIOR ESSENTIALS	9781636513263
DIGITAL MARKETING ESSENTIALS	9781949395747
MARKETING MANAGEMENT ESSENTIALS	9781636511788
MARKET RESEARCH ESSENTIALS	9781636513744
SALES MANAGEMENT ESSENTIALS	9781636510743
SERVICES MARKETING ESSENTIALS	9781636511733
SOCIAL MEDIA MARKETING ESSENTIALS	9781636512181

*Also available in Hardback & Ebook formats

SELF-LEARNING MANAGEMENT SERIES

TITLE	PAPERBACK* ISBN
OPERATIONS MANAGEMENT	
AGILE ESSENTIALS	9781636510057
OPERATIONS & SUPPLY CHAIN MANAGEMENT ESSENTIALS	9781949395242
PROJECT MANAGEMENT ESSENTIALS	9781636510712
STAKEHOLDER ENGAGEMENT ESSENTIALS	9781636511511
CURRENT AFFAIRS	
DIGITAL SHOCK	9781636513805

*Also available in Hardback & Ebook formats

This page is intentionally left blank

About the Author

Pablo Ibarreche is an executive with over 25 years of expertise in marketing and management across Latin America and Europe. He has showcased his skills starting from his days in the sports retail industry at Sporting in Argentina to holding brand management positions at P&G, Citibank, and AIG Insurance. During his time in Europe, he engaged in consulting work related to franchising. Upon returning to Argentina he currently holds the position of President at Alsa Commercial Real Estate, acts as the Chief Revenue Manager for Reforest Latam, and works as a business consultant.

Additionally, he has shared his knowledge as an international marketing professor at institutions such as Ucema Buenos Aires, UNT Tucuman, and PUC Valparaiso in Chile. He is part of the MBA graduating thesis examination board at Universidad Siglo XXI, Cordoba, Argentina. Fluent in three languages, Pablo earned a Bachelor's degree in Administration from UNT Argentina. Pursued an MBA, at J.L. Kellogg School of Management, Northwestern University.

This page is intentionally left blank

What experts say about this book!

Consumer Behavior Essentials You Always Wanted to Know is a comprehensive overview of marketing. It covers key topics in an easy-to-follow manner and includes relevant, recognizable examples to bring them to life. Each chapter contains a quiz and a convenient recap to help readers retain key information. Students and practitioners alike will find the book a valuable resource that can be referred to often.

– Nancy Harhut, Chief Creative Officer, HBT Marketing
Author, Using Behavioral Science in Marketing

Consumer Behaviour Essentials provides a comprehensive and accessible introduction to the field of consumer behavior. The book breaks down key concepts, theories, and models in a way that is engaging for both students and professionals. It covers the psychological, social, and cultural factors that influence consumer decisions, offering valuable insights into how consumers make choices in today's complex marketplace.

The text is well-structured, with clear explanations, real-world examples, and case studies that illustrate the practical applications of consumer behavior theory. One of its strengths is the ability to blend foundational principles with modern trends, such as the impact of digital media and sustainability on consumer choices. The book also includes relevant data and research, providing a solid foundation for further study or professional practice.

Overall, Consumer Behaviour Essentials is a useful resource for anyone looking to understand the underlying motivations behind consumer actions and the ways businesses can adapt to meet their needs effectively.

– Pratik Chauhan, Assistant Professor,
VIDYABHARTI TRUST COLLEGE OF MCA-MBA

This page is intentionally left blank

Table of Contents

This page is intentionally left blank

Preface

In the 1990s, as I started my first job in the world of marketing, I observed an evolution similar to that of fields like medicine. Nowadays marketing is predominantly driven by science with a touch of artistry. Let me share a tale I often narrate to my students. Imagine a village healer once labeled as a witch, who relied on tradition and beliefs to cure ailments in the community. As time passed, science gradually seeped into the practices replacing myths and traditions with proven methods and trial-and-error approaches that ultimately led to a methodology. Today those mystical healers are no more; instead, we have dedicated physicians who follow established protocols and base their knowledge on tested and proven techniques.

Drawing parallels to marketing we have evolved from being perceived as "witches" in our craft to becoming marketing scientists. We now adhere to protocols that distinguish strategies from ones through continuous testing and learning processes. Is there room for creativity? Absolutely. All business is not a science; it allows for some degree of improvisation despite witnessing occasional industry upheavals that are more exceptions than norms.

So what's the aim of this book? It explores the realm of consumer behavior—a domain where various scientific disciplines intersect seamlessly.

My first meeting with a consumer behavior professor who came from a sociology background was both fascinating and invigorating. He wasn't alone; there were others from fields like psychology, psychiatry, mathematics, and business who all played roles in studying consumer behavior.

I strive to approach consumer behavior from different angles and offer insights for all readers. The goal is to empower them to use this knowledge to create customers and ultimately strengthen their financial standing. Isn't that the essence of being in this industry? Wishing you the best, on your journey!

Introduction to the book

In the changing world of marketing, understanding consumer behavior is, like having a compass that guides businesses through the world of customer preferences. Just as medicine has evolved from healing practices to science, marketing has transitioned from mystical arts to a structured field governed by proven strategies and methods. Picture consumer behavior as the core element of your marketing plan influencing every aspect of your strategy.

From the role of consumer behavior in shaping your marketing approach to the psychological and social factors that influence our decisions each chapter reveals a deeper level of insight. We navigate through the decision-making journey uncovering the stages from awareness to building long-term relationships and shedding light on the complexities that drive our choices.

As we step into the marketplace we see the landscape of consumer behavior emerging. Cultural details play a role in defining target audiences making market research essential for deciphering these details.

The visible indicators in service industries are manifested in "Physical Evidence " highlighting the significance of a link to services. The concept of "Partnerships" is highlighted, underscoring collaboration as a component in achieving objectives.

Furthermore, we elaborate on the increasing focus on "Purpose" in marketing. This strategy involves aligning the brand with a purpose or social responsibility nurturing a bond with consumers who are increasingly drawn to brands that make a meaningful impact.

In impactful language, this book aims to provide you with insights into navigating the evolving landscape of consumer behavior promoting satisfaction, loyalty, and ultimately success in the market. Welcome to a domain where science and creativity intersect to study the enigmas of the consumer's psyche—a journey that holds promise, for being as enlightening as it is essential.

Who can benefit from this book?

This book aims to provide insights and practical knowledge to a range of readers. Here are the types of people who could gain from exploring consumer behavior within its pages;

1. **College students**

   - Students studying marketing and business can acquire an understanding of consumer behavior laying the groundwork for future marketing pursuits.

   - Those in sociology and psychology fields will get to delve into the aspects of consumer behavior and its ties to sciences.

2. **Entrepreneurs**

   - Individuals starting their businesses can learn how to grasp and utilize consumer behavior for product development and marketing.

   - Owners of businesses can create strategies for attracting and retaining customers fostering business expansion.

3. **Corporate executives and managers**

   - Marketing executives can enhance planning by integrating insights on consumer behavior into campaigns and initiatives.

   - Sales managers can use the book to comprehend customer motivations and decision-making processes to optimize sales tactics.

4. Business leaders can gain a view of consumer behavior to guide organizational decision-making processes and boost customer satisfaction.

How to use this book?

1. **Engage in learning:** Interact with the content. Ponder over the case studies, stories, and real-world examples provided. Consider how these concepts relate to your experiences whether you're a student, entrepreneur, executive, or marketing.

2. **Apply the concepts in real life:** Implement the knowledge acquired in real-world situations. Whether you're creating a marketing strategy, refining a product, or designing an advertising campaign, use the principles discussed in each chapter to guide your decision-making process.

3. **Create groups for discussions:** Spark discussions, by sharing takeaways with peers, colleagues, or classmates. Consumer behavior is ever-changing and collaborative discussions can bring perspectives and insights.

4. **Utilize the hands-on activities hands-on activities:** Make use of exercises and reflection questions at the end of each chapter. These activities are meant to reinforce learning and promote application.

5. **Refer to specific sections:** If you have an area of interest or need to tackle a challenge, feel free to skip ahead to the relevant sections. Each chapter is designed to stand offering insights and practical strategies.

Keep this book handy, as a go-to guide. Whenever you face challenges or opportunities in your professional path, revisit relevant sections to refresh your knowledge and find motivation.

If you're an educator, think about tailoring the content to suit your audience. Customize case studies, examples, and discussions to match your student's interests and backgrounds.

Don't forget to check out the resources recommended throughout the book. These could include readings, online courses, or more case studies that will deepen your understanding of topics.

Remember to share your thoughts and learnings, with the author and other readers. Consumer behavior is always. Your insights play a role in the ongoing dialogue. Embrace a mindset of learning and adaptation.

By following these suggestions you can turn this book from a read into a practical tool that will enhance your grasp of consumer behavior and empower you to make informed decisions in the intricate world of marketing. Enjoy the journey!

This page is intentionally left blank

Chapter **1**

What is Consumer Behavior? Definition, Scope, and Evolution

The opening chapter delves into the realm of consumer behavior (CB) shedding light on its meaning, extent, and development. It explores the emergence of CB and discusses different viewpoints, theories, and methods related to the subject. The aim is to clarify for readers the definition, evolutionary path, conflicting perspectives, fundamental aspects, and obstacles encountered in CB. This chapter lays down a groundwork for understanding customer behavior, paving the way for a detailed examination of the factors impacting and steering consumer decisions in today's market landscape.

Key learning objectives should include the reader's understanding of the following:

- The definition of customer behavior
- The multifaceted scope of consumer behavior
- The evolution of consumer behavior over time
- Interdisciplinary roots of consumer behavior

1.1 Defining Consumer Behavior

Well, here we are, the starting point! Let's begin by getting a basic understanding of consumer behavior and then we can delve into its intricacies.

Consumer behavior should be defined here, and we would like to have a definition that is as pragmatic, inclusive, and simple as possible. Let's imagine we are a company creating a marketing plan for our products. Consumer behavior is simply how a group of people will behave in front of our marketing plan and its execution. What exactly do they do with our products and their information? Do they know we exist? Do they like our product? If so, when and how will they buy it? Are they going to become repeat buyers, or will it just be a one-time deal? How can we have them come back more often and buy our products for a higher price tag if possible? And lastly, are they fans of our product, or are they looking for new alternatives? These, and many other questions, revolve around the behavior of our consumers and how we can manage this process from a marketing standpoint.

We all agree that we are looking for profitability and sales in the business world. So, consumer behavior is defined based on the result of this bottom line. Simply put, consumer behavior is understanding customers' behavior in order to drive sales.

If we remember high school mathematics, we can imagine consumer behavior to be a function with many variables such as age, sex, and marital status of the group, to name a few. The result we want is sales—or, better yet, profitability. Whatever happens in these variables will impact sales, and these variables are part of consumer behavior.

For example, imagine you are booking a plane flight from New York to Buenos Aires as a tourist and you have some flexibility regarding departing and returning days and hours. You start looking for alternatives in Kayak, an excellent online searching/booking service. Kayak shows you the "recommended" flights based on a certain algorithm. You can see that you can buy the cheapest flight if you select flights from lowest cost to higher cost, but you discover that it may depart at 3 am. Or maybe it flies you to Bogota first, Lima, and then to Buenos Aires, with a total flight time of more than 30 hours. Some tickets do not include ticketed luggage, and some have no free food on board. Some flights use Boeing 737s, and others use much larger aircraft.

To summarize, there are so many options available for so many different consumer behaviors. One of the options will be the best option for you. It may be the cheapest one. It may be your favorite airline. Or the one that adds miles to your account. In this example, the success (or sales) of Kayak, the booking service, depends on selecting the consumer group that best fits their service and marketing to them based on their behavior.

Thus we understand that success (or sales) depends on selecting the best-fit consumer group. Is it essential that this group is large? It may be necessary. Maybe it is more important that they are underserved so that you are the winner. This is a consumer behavior/mathematics game. We will do our best to give you tools in this exciting process of charting consumer behaviors for your business or idea.

As we delve deeper, remember that understanding consumer behavior is not a standalone pursuit; it's intricately linked to the success of your broader marketing plan. Consumer choices are the driving force that propels your strategies forward and ultimately shapes your business outcomes.

Join us in this exciting process of decoding consumer behaviors as we equip you with tools and insights to navigate the dynamic marketplace and foster success for your business or idea. Let's embark on this journey together!

1.2 The Multifaceted Scope of Consumer Behavior

Understanding how consumers behave is exactly the same as solving a puzzle in the world of business and marketing. Consumer behavior is not about making purchases; it involves a mix of psychological factors, brand preferences, and responses to various marketing strategies. In this exploration, we go into the layers of this field examining the details that influence how people interact with products and brands.

1.2.1 Purchasing choices: More than just transactions

Consumer behavior studies the decisions individuals make when purchasing goods or services. It goes beyond the act of buying itself; it's about understanding the reasoning, motivations, and factors that influence consumers throughout their buying journey. From recognizing a need to completing a purchase, each stage reflects influences that businesses need to understand to tailor their strategies.

Let's take Amazon as an example. In the changing world of online retail, Amazon stands out as a company that excels in catering to impulsive buying tendencies. The seamless browsing experience and one-click purchasing option create an environment for decision-making.

Amazon is really good at understanding what makes people buy things on a whim, using things like limited-time deals and personalized suggestions. The big online store has become known for satisfying our desire for gratification when we make purchases, proving that a well-designed online platform can successfully navigate and take advantage of how consumers behave in today's digital world.

1.2.2 Brand preferences: The emotional side of loyalty

Consumer behavior also plays a role in the brands the consumers prefer when they form connections with companies. This aspect explores why consumers are attracted to brands, creating loyalty that goes beyond just the product itself. Brand preferences are influenced by factors such as brand image, values, and the overall experience associated with a brand.

Take Apple for instance. They have built a brand identity that goes beyond their products. Their sleek designs, user interfaces, and sense of exclusivity all contribute to a customer base that often goes beyond logical reasons.

1.2.3 Responses to marketing tactics: Navigating through the world of influence

In today's world of information overload, consumer behavior is heavily impacted by all sorts of marketing messages bombarding us. This aspect explores how people react to marketing approaches from advertising, to online campaigns and social media interactions. Businesses need to figure out what connects with their target audience and adjust their approach accordingly.

For instance, take a look at social media influencer marketing. The increasing popularity of social media influencers showcases how marketing trends are changing. Younger consumers tend to react to genuine endorsements from influencers they admire.

For example, in the world of soccer, Lionel Messi's global influence goes beyond boundaries, contributing to the sport's expansion in the US. As soccer gains momentum Messi's star quality captures attention among people. By embracing influencer marketing principles within soccer, it not only capitalizes on his appeal but also harnesses the influence of relatable influencers who resonate with America's diverse and growing soccer community. This fusion of Messi's influence and influencer-driven marketing signifies a period for soccer's presence in the US, shaping an environment where the sport flourishes both on and off the field.

To conclude, in navigating consumer behavior complexities, businesses encounter both hurdles and chances for growth. By delving into consumers purchasing decisions, brand preferences, and responses to marketing strategies, companies can customize their approaches to cater to the needs and expectations of their audience.

Exploring the world of consumer behavior is an adventure that demands flexibility and a profound grasp of the elements influencing people's choices in a constantly evolving market.

1.3 Evolution Over Time

Understanding customer behavior has transitioned from rudimentary to sophisticated science in the ever-evolving business and marketing landscape. The journey from early insights to contemporary approaches showcases the dynamic nature of consumer interactions and unveils how businesses adapt to changing trends.

1.3.1 Early insights: A glimpse into the past

In the early days of business, understanding customer behavior was akin to deciphering an ancient script—limited data, basic observations, and a reliance on intuition. Merchants engage with customers face-to-face and build relationships based on personal interactions and trust. While this human-centric approach had its merits, it lacked the systematic methodologies that characterize modern consumer behavior studies.

1.3.2 The rise of market research: Mid-20th century

In the 1950s, market researchers started incorporating some elements of science in their works. This also marks the beginning of businesses utilizing interviews, surveys, and other tools for observational studies to collect useful qualitative and quantitative data on consumer preferences. It was during this period that Ernest Dichter became quite popular as a pioneer in applying psychological theories to understanding consumer behaviors. His efforts and those of others contributed to the commencement of scientific market research.

In his initial market research for General Motors, Ernest Dichter incredibly demonstrated that cars could indicate more than just a means of transportation but also an object symbolizing status, personal identity, and freedom. Dichter discovered that some consumers preferred car models that reflected their emotional excitement and personal success or achievement, thereby associating some special cars with personality characteristics. The automotive industry then was obviously revolutionized by this new marketing perspective as car dealers concentrated more on consumers' emotional appeal rather than technical specifications such as a car's fuel efficiency and performance. This prompted a new kind of advertising when companies began to draft marketing campaigns that were mostly focusing on consumers' desires and preferences/tastes.

Ernest Dichter's work can be regarded as the basis on which modern marketing is built, emphasizing connecting with consumers emotionally and personally to influence their buying decisions.

1.3.3 Behavioral economics and the cognitive turn

The late 20th century ushered in behavioral economics that had, in principle, transformed advertising/marketing in those days and now. Prominent behavioral economics scholars such as Daniel Kahneman and Amos Tversky revealed that consumers often rely on their psychological biases when making certain decisions, including buying decisions. This cognitive turn, as they pointed out, was responsible for consumers making important decisions based on their emotions and perceptions rather than on merits and rational reasoning or logic.

In behavioral economics, the term "anchoring effect" denotes a cognitive bias that describes the human habit of depending heavily on the first piece of information passed across to them ("the anchor"), and then using that information to make the final judgments. Amazon is one of the leading companies adopting the "anchoring effect" to improve customer experience, increase conversions, drive sales, and increase revenues by encouraging consumers to make favorable buying decisions. Amazon applies the "anchoring effect" in its product pricing. On Amazon's product page, consumers can see the initial real price (anchor) of the product they are interested in as well as a recommended/discounted price beside it. This gives consumers the feeling that the discounted price is a good deal/bargain; so, they will quickly order the product using the recommended price.

Amazon mostly used the "anchoring effect" in its time-limited discount sales such as Amazon's "Deal of the Day" or "Lightning Deals". When shoppers notice the discounted prices beside the higher prices, it creates a sense of urgency in them and causes them to make buying decisions quickly.

Amazon also displays its products conspicuously so that customers can easily identify the different prices (both the initial and recommended prices) and immediately decide to purchase whatever product they are interested in. This approach gives Amazon the opportunity to discover how shoppers usually respond to its pricing strategy.

Amazon continues to adopt this behavioral economics concept to streamline online shopping for its customers and boosts its sales along the way.

1.3.4 The digital revolution: A game-changer

The digital revolution can be credited for bringing organizations and their customers together, erasing the distance or divide that used to exist between them. Nowadays, it is possible for consumers to shop online through e-commerce or social media without leaving the comfort of their sofas or couches.

Businesses, on the other hand, track their customers' activities online using real-time analytics. This approach gives businesses a new dimension of gathering useful information about their customers and using their findings to influence their behaviors and shopping experiences. The insights obtainable from the collected data provide clear indications about the consumers' shopping patterns, encouraging companies to intensify their interactions with their customers through the following digital approaches:

- **Social media integration:** Fashion Nova, for example, utilizes the power of social media integration to drive traffic and, of course, potential customers to its e-commerce platform via its Instagram account.

- **Increased engagement through personalized marketing:** With its *NikeRun* membership program, Nike leverages personalized marketing approaches to provide its members with the customized content they require, exclusive offers, and early access to newly launched products.

- **E-commerce platform:** To ensure that its customers are well served, Stitch Fix, an online business that offers personal styling services, provides clothing selections based on each customer's preferences.

The above-mentioned examples highlight how businesses are utilizing their knowledge of consumer behavior to serve their customers better by providing customized services, personalized e-commerce, and using advanced technologies and insights from behavioral economics to quickly respond to changes in consumers' trends and preferences.

1.3.5 Contemporary approaches: Integrating multiple disciplines

In today's world, the study of customer behavior has evolved into a domain drawing inspiration from psychology, sociology, neuroscience, and data science. By integrating fields of study companies, like Google and Facebook aim to understand the factors influencing consumer decisions.

Google heavily relies on insights from disciplines to comprehend user behavior. By analyzing search patterns, click-through rates, and user engagement with products and services Google applies principles from psychology and data science to enhance user experience, customize advertisements, and improve its range of services.

Similarly, Facebook utilizes an interesting approach to understanding user behavior as a social media platform. Integrating psychology and sociology in its operations allows Facebook to optimize algorithms for delivering personalized content targeted advertisements and enhanced user interactions. Data science plays a role at Facebook by enabling the analysis of vast amounts of user-generated data for precise advertising strategies and content suggestions.

Companies like Neuro Insight study neuromarketing as a field that merges neuroscience with marketing concepts. Through measuring brain activity responses in consumers Neuro Insight gains insights into how individuals react to marketing stimuli on a level. This information assists companies, including known brands in grasping the foundations of consumer decisions enabling them to develop marketing strategies that are more impactful and memorable.

By combining perspectives from fields businesses are empowered to obtain an understanding of consumer behavior. Whether it's Google and Facebook leveraging psychology and data analysis, for user interactions or Neuro-Insight using neuroscience to reveal the complexities of consumer decisions these firms demonstrate how a diverse approach improves their capacity to effectively connect with consumers in today's market landscape.

1.4 Interdisciplinary Roots

Studying customer behavior involves integrating insights, from fields like psychology, sociology, and economics. By combining these disciplines, we can better understand how people engage with products and brands.

Figure 1.1 Interdisciplinary roots of consumer behavior

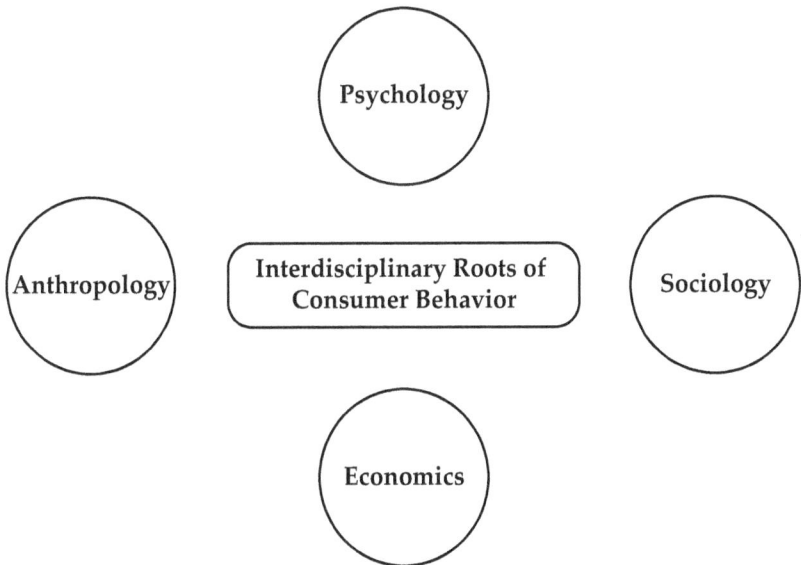

1.4.1 Psychology in consumer behavior

Psychology plays a role in discovering customer behavior by going deep into the intricacies of the mind. Psychologists study motivations, perceptions, and decision-making processes to grasp how emotions and attitudes influence consumer choices.

The concept of loss aversion, popularized by psychologists like Daniel Kahneman illustrates that individuals often prioritize avoiding losses over gaining benefits when making purchasing decisions.

Businesses leverage this idea by presenting discounts as a means to prevent losses rather than focusing on price cuts. For instance, if a product is 20% cheaper they might phrase it as "Don't miss out on this 20% discount!" This approach underscores the sense of missing out on the discount rather than solely highlighting the price or presenting the upside of buying cheaper than you would. Another prevalent practice in the software industry is the known concept of "freeware." Many companies offer free trial versions of their subscription services to attract users. When individuals try a service for free they may develop an attachment to it making it challenging for them to cancel the subscription even if they initially had no intention of paying for it. Free trials essentially play on the fear of losing something to users like access they have grown used to if they choose not to participate.

1.4.2 Sociology in consumer behavior

Examining interactions is crucial for understanding how people are influenced by their surroundings. Elements such as norms, cultural values, and group dynamics impact how consumers make decisions. By understanding these factors businesses can tailor their strategies to effectively resonate with communities. For example, in sociology, social identity theory highlights how individuals derive their identities from group affiliations which influence their brand preferences and consumption patterns.

To delve deeper into this concept let's consider two examples:

1. **Coca-Cola:** Embracing cultural diversity

   Coca-Cola is known for creating marketing campaigns that connect with backgrounds. The company acknowledges the role of norms and cultural values in shaping consumer choices. Initiatives like "Share a Coke" demonstrate inclusivity and draw upon identity theory. By personalizing Coke bottles with names and cultural references, Coca-Cola fosters a sense of belonging and personal connection that aligns with consumers' social identities.

2. **Ben & Jerry's:** Embracing responsibility, in branding

Ben & Jerry's Ice Cream has built a brand around principles that emphasize responsibility and community engagement. The company understands how societal norms impact consumer behavior.

Ben & Jerry's commitment to justice, environmental sustainability, and fair trade resonates with consumers who prioritize such brands. This demonstrates how being mindful of these values can cultivate brand loyalty.

1.4.3 Exploring economics and behavior

While economics focuses on decision-making processes, it also delves into understanding consumer behavior. Behavioral economics merges principles with psychology to recognize that consumers often make decisions based on factors beyond rationality. The research of Nobel laureate Richard Thaler in economics sheds light on how individuals exhibit rationality and are influenced by biases challenging the view of completely rational decision-making.

Amazon's dynamic pricing algorithms and transparent practices serve as examples of these concepts in action. Amazon utilizes pricing tactics rooted in principles by adjusting prices based on shopping patterns over time. By maintaining communication and promptly adapting prices, Amazon effectively manages consumer reactions, challenging beliefs and aligning with the complexities of decision-making processes. For insights into Amazon's implementation of this strategy please refer to the case study provided at the end of this chapter.

1.4.4 Anthropology: Understanding cultural influences

The field of anthropology offers insights into the factors shaping consumer behavior. By studying anthropology businesses can gain an understanding of how rituals, symbols, and traditions impact purchasing choices, within communities. Recognizing these nuances empowers companies to develop tailored marketing approaches that resonate authentically with audiences.

Unilever's Dove brand is an example of this idea, known for its sensitivity. They use anthropology to create personal care products that fit norms and beauty standards. Dove customizes its products and marketing to match beauty preferences, around the world enhancing the brand's appeal and building connections with consumers globally.

Marketing acts as a bridge blending insights from fields to develop strategies. In marketing research knowledge from psychology, sociology, economics, and other disciplines is combined to understand consumer behavior. By analyzing why consumers make decisions and segmenting markets based on factors like age and income businesses can implement pricing strategies rooted in theories.

Taking an approach allows businesses to tailor their offerings based on an understanding of consumer behavior influences. By recognizing the interconnected nature of psychology, sociology, economics, anthropology, and marketing companies can navigate the changing consumer landscape with depth and insight. This interdisciplinary foundation sets the stage for businesses seeking to comprehend and shape consumer behavior dynamics in a market that is constantly evolving.

Quiz

1. **Consumer behavior is defined as _____.**
    a. Actions and responses to marketing efforts
    b. Brand preferences
    c. Purchasing decisions
    d. None of the above

2. **The emphasis of consumer behavior is on _____.**
    a. Enhancing brand loyalty
    b. Maximizing market share
    c. Enhancing profitability and sales
    d. None of the above

3. **Consumer behavior draws insights from which discipline?**
    a. Sociology
    b. Economics
    c. Psychology
    d. All of the above

4. **Who is a notable figure in consumer behavior research?**
    a. Daniel Kahneman
    b. Philip Kotler
    c. Ernest Dichter
    d. None of the above

5. **Consumer behavior extends beyond _____.**
    a. Purchasing decisions
    b. Impulse buying
    c. Brand preferences
    d. None of the above

6. **Amazon is known for its mastery in** _____.
    a. Brand building
    b. Customer service
    c. Impulse buying
    d. None of the above

7. **Apple is known for its** _____.
    a. Cultural resonance
    b. Market saturation
    c. Product innovation
    d. None of the above

8. **Consumer behavior goes beyond just buying decisions by also analyzing** _____.
    a. Brand awareness only
    b. Customer service experiences
    c. Advertising recall
    d. Product features solely

9. **Choosing a plane ticket exemplifies the complex decision-making process involved in** _____.
    a. All purchases
    b. Only luxury goods
    c. Primarily impulse purchases
    d. Solely everyday necessities

10. **Factors influencing consumer behavior can include** _____.

   a. Age and income only

   b. Cultural background and social norms

   c. Advertising messages alone

   d. Brand logos solely

Answers	1 – c	2 – c	3 – c	4 – a	5 – d
	6 – c	7 – c	8 – b	9 – a	10 – b

Chapter Summary

◆ Consumer behavior isn't just about buying decisions, it also includes how people react to marketing efforts and their brand choices.

◆ Multiple factors like age and gender influence consumer behavior, making it a complex field.

◆ Studies go beyond purchases and analyze brand choices and responses to marketing. Companies like Amazon (impulse buying) and Apple (brand loyalty) show this.

◆ The field has evolved from basic insights to modern research methods like market research and behavioral economics. Pioneering figures like Dichter and Kahneman played a key role in shaping our understanding.

◆ A holistic view is essential. Consumer behavior research integrates psychology, sociology, economics, and anthropology to understand consumer choices.

Further Reading

Refer to the following videos to enhance understanding of the concepts and examples discussed in this chapter. Links to these videos are also available in the Online Resources section of this book.

- Ernest Dichter - Motivational Research: https://www.youtube.com/watch?v=qALfP8zeSdg

- The Anchoring Effect: https://www.youtube.com/watch?v=igv_O-azRUc

- The New Nike Run app: https://www.youtube.com/watch?v=HF-bV1Lar1k

- Neuromarketing: The new science of consumer decisions | Terry Wu | TEDxBlaine: https://www.youtube.com/watch?v=UEtE-el6KKs

- Impulsive shopping: https://www.youtube.com/watch?v=cF2UzT0TCBA

- Messi will help us build soccer, by Adidas president: https://www.youtube.com/watch?v=dRLv2Aotk2A

- Share a Coke campaign in the USA: https://www.youtube.com/watch?v=5-ahnFYzMp8

- Dove's Toxic Influence - A film: https://www.youtube.com/watch?v=sF3iRZtkyAQ

Case Study: Amazon as an example of Behavioral Economics

This case study dives into how Amazon mastered behavioral economics using the following strategies:

1. **Personalized pricing models:**

   One of the critical principles in behavioral economics is the acknowledgment that consumers sometimes make decisions based on relaxed rationality. As a pioneer in e-commerce, Amazon recognizes this and incorporates personalized pricing models.

   Amazon's algorithms analyze many factors, including user browsing history, past purchases, and real-time demand, to determine individual product prices. This goes beyond traditional economic models, where prices are often assumed to be uniform for all consumers.

2. **Addressing bounded rationality:**

   Nobel Laureate Herbert A. Simon proposed that owing to certain cognitive limitations on the part of some people, they equally exhibit limited decision-making capabilities.

   In the context of Amazon's pricing strategy, this means understanding that consumers may only sometimes have complete information or make optimal choices.

   By adjusting prices dynamically, Amazon accounts for the limited information available to consumers. The platform adapts to the bounded rationality of users by presenting prices influenced by factors like current demand or the user's historical interactions, fostering a pricing strategy that aligns with realistic decision-making constraints.

3. Transparent communication:

Transparency and communication are crucial elements in behavioral economics to mitigate adverse consumer reactions. Understanding the psychological aspects of pricing perception is essential.

Amazon employs clear communication strategies during dynamic pricing scenarios, explaining the reasons behind price fluctuations. By providing transparency, the company aims to manage consumer expectations and reduce the perceived unfairness that might arise due to changing prices. This aligns with behavioral economics insights into how consumers respond to information and framing.

4. Real-time adaptations:

Behavioral economics emphasizes the importance of real-time adaptations to consumer behavior. Traditional economic models might not account for decision-making's dynamic and context-dependent nature.

Amazon's algorithms continuously adapt to real-time changes in demand, external factors, and user behavior. This dynamic approach ensures that the platform remains responsive to fluctuations in consumer preferences and market conditions, reflecting an understanding of consumer decisions' evolving and sometimes irrational nature.

In summary, it can be deduced that Amazon has revolutionized online shopping by developing algorithms that utilize data about consumers' behavioral patterns or behavioral economics to predict and personalize prices and customize customer services in real-time, actively engaging consumers with prompt communication, guidance, and shopping recommendations.

Discussion

1. **Transparency vs. privacy concerns**

   Amazon emphasizes transparency in its dynamic pricing through explanations for price fluctuations. However, the concept of personalized pricing also raises privacy concerns. How can Amazon effectively balance the need for transparency in pricing with the need to protect user privacy?

   This question digs deeper into the potential tension between providing consumers with information about price changes and the amount of user data collected to personalize those prices. It prompts discussion about how Amazon can strike a balance between these two aspects.

2. **Impact on consumer choice and market competition**

   Amazon's dynamic pricing strategy can influence consumer purchasing decisions. How might this approach affect competition within the e-commerce market? Could it potentially lead to a situation where smaller businesses struggle to compete with Amazon's dynamic pricing tactics? Discuss the potential benefits and drawbacks for consumers and the broader market.

3. **The future of dynamic pricing and consumer behavior**

   As technology advances, personalized pricing models will likely become even more sophisticated. How might this trend impact consumer behavior in the long run? Will consumers become accustomed to dynamic pricing and adapt their shopping strategies accordingly? Could it lead to a future where traditional, fixed pricing becomes less common? Discuss the potential implications for both consumers and businesses in this evolving landscape.

Chapter **2**

Consumer Behavior in a Marketing Plan

Chapter two elaborates on the symbiotic relationship between consumer behavior and a well-crafted marketing plan. It underscores the necessity of defining both the marketing plan and the target market behavior, highlighting their integral roles in driving business success. Emphasizing the importance of a precise and competitive definition, the chapter explores how these definitions evolve over time. Analogizing consumer behavior definition to a steering wheel, it elucidates that its significance lies in its integration within the broader framework of the marketing plan. The chapter sets the stage for subsequent discussions on target market definition, recognizing its pivotal role in shaping the marketing plan's trajectory.

Key learning objectives should include the reader's understanding of the following:

- The meaning of a marketing plan
- The parts of a marketing plan
- SWOT analysis and its importance

2.1 What is a Marketing Plan?

To define a marketing plan, we must first understand a few issues. For a marketing plan to exist, you must first find a sizable market where you can profitably satisfy a specific need.

2.1.1 Needs

A need is a "discovery" of a necessity that some people or organizations have, even if they are unaware they have it. Let me give you an example, a simple one. Humankind walked barefoot for centuries. One day, somebody invented "something" to cover people's feet and protect their feet. This probably happened one day, giving some people an advantage over others in their quest for food or defense purposes. When humans saw this invention, which we will call the shoe (it probably was not a shoe but some leaves tied to the foot), they recognized that they had a "need," and now there was a product to fix this need. This new product enables its users to run more miles, have less damage to their feet, and walk more hours, among many benefits.

When television was invented, consumers did not know they needed to buy it. They did need to be entertained, though. This need was covered by radio, reading, playing games, conversation with family and next-door neighbors, like my grandmother used to do. TV was more fun than next-door neighbors! So TV was a huge success. Now we have so many entertainment options! If you had asked consumers if they needed TikTok to be entertained before it was launched, they would have said no. Unless, as marketing research theory knows, the consumers test the product concept themselves, they won't know they need it. This is part of a subsequent chapter. In summary, needs exist, and marketers find new and exciting ways to cover them.

Needs are never created. They are there to be discovered. It would be fantastic if we, marketers, could create needs. We would be millionaires selling bricks to be worn on top of people's heads!

This does not happen. A marketer or an inventor will find a pre-existing need and create something to solve this. What solves people's needs are called products, services, or ideas.

A product is something physical to solve a need. A service is something intangible to solve a need. A hat is a product. Cleaning your house for a fee is a service. Finally, an idea is a service that fixes a need but does not require payment.

2.1.2 Market

Now what is a market? A market is a group of individuals with a need and money to pay for it. As a simple definition, if you do not have money, you may need shoes but you cannot buy them, so we do not have a market in marketing terms. This may not be right or morally correct, but that is frequently the reality of our world.

If we have a product that fixes a need and a market that can pay for it, let us imagine we have a rectangle. Inside it, there are consumers, all of them with a need and money. And we have a product/service/idea. Outside this market, some people either do not have a need (at least in our definition) or need more money to pay for it.

This rectangle, which represents our market, will always be divided into smaller parts. These parts are called segments. Segments are the parts in which a market is divided. How is that? You can have the US car market, and each segment can be a State. Why is that? If you need to sell to these segments by tweaking your offer at least a bit, then these segments must be treated separately. Again, in the American market, one segment is New York, and the second is New Jersey. Why is that? Because you need dealers close to where people buy! Different dealers, different segments.

A segment is a part of the total market that requires a specific market offer to improve sales. This is basically a "marketing plan". There you are. We have reached the definition of a marketing plan, at least a simple one.

We need to address one crucial definition, too. What is marketing? Marketing is the process of creating and executing a product, service, or idea to satisfy a need in a person or organization, including the famous 4 Ps in it: the **product** itself (or service or idea), its **price**, its **promotion** or communication, and its **place** or marketing channel. We say marketing is a process because it is active: we define a starting point, final objective, and measures for the plan's success. Remember that marketing an idea will carry no P for the price, though.

2.2 The Parts of a Marketing Plan

A marketing plan is a document where an organization will write what it intends to do with a product, a line of products, a brand, or multiple brands in a coordinated corporate strategy. It is a fantastic effort where all involved parties get to share a point of view towards a common objective. Normally, general management asks for a marketing plan and executives will show how much money they are going to require, how they are going to use it, and what type of return they are going to get, all speaking not in financial but in marketing terms.

Imagine that you are assigned a brand. A general manager tells you that you will be a brand manager for Doritos in Perú. A marketing plan will be required of you as to who is going to buy the product, your competition, prices, and promotions, among many other issues. Doritos will be sold in a shared channel by a staff that is going to sell other brands too. A marketing plan has to have this type of issue included. So, in this example, we have already included the opinion and approval of finance and sales. Logistics will also be there, along with legal affairs, production, and HR, among many others. In summary, a marketing plan is a corporate effort with a focus on a brand, or a product within a brand.

A marketing plan serves as a blueprint for businesses to navigate their marketing activities effectively. A comprehensive marketing plan typically includes several essential components that collectively guide the organization's marketing efforts. While specific structures may vary, the fundamental parts often have:

1. **Executive summary:** As its name implies, it is a succinct summary of the main marketing plan's contents. Stakeholders can quickly extract vital information about the strategies, processes, and procedures an organization will be employing to achieve its goals/objectives.

2. **Business overview:** This section provides cogent and important information about the organization, including its business operations, mission and vision, market position, and organizational values. It also includes brief information about the organization's goals, profile, and modus operandi. It is possible to use these pieces of information to create a customized marketing plan that will advance the organization's objectives.

3. **Market analysis:** This section highlights all the essential market analysis procedures or steps that the organization will take to critically analyze its industry, strengths, markets, competitors, weaknesses, available opportunities, and threats.

4. **Target audience:** It is expected that before an organization can create effective marketing campaigns, it must fully understand its target audience's behaviors or characteristics, demographics, buying patterns or trends, psychographics, and preferences.

5. **Marketing goals and objectives:** Information about the organization's marketing objectives can be obtained from this section. It may be advisable to apply the SMART (Specific, Measurable, Achievable, Relevant, and Time-bound) marketing model to the organization's marketing goals in a way that is compatible with its values and visions.

6. **Marketing strategies:** This section highlights the different marketing strategies that the organization wants to adopt in its marketing campaigns. It will also reveal the organization's

types of marketing communications, branding, and positioning in order to fully make judicious use of the available resources while paying attention to the 4Ps of marketing, namely product, place, price, and promotion.

7. **Action plans:** The action plans will reveal the steps and procedures that the organization will take in undertaking every aspect of its marketing drive. It may also be necessary to describe the applicable roles and responsibilities to be executed by each team member. There will equally be timelines apportioned to the completion of each marketing process.

8. **Budget:** Every marketing plan has a budget dedicated to achieving all the marketing and operational goals highlighted in the plan. It is important to ensure that the organization has adequate funds for a marketing campaign before embarking on it. Otherwise, a shoddily executed marketing campaign may eventually flop or fail.

9. **Metrics and Key Performance Indicators (KPIs):** KPIs such as sales figures, conversion rates, revenue rates, customer acquisition costs, etc. are necessary to determine the effectiveness of a marketing strategy. They are usually included in a marketing plan.

10. **Implementation schedule:** Every marketing campaign is expected to be completed within a specific timeline or schedule. Since funds and resources are sometimes an issue for organizations, it is important to maximize funds and properly manage resource allocation through effective scheduling.

11. **Monitoring and evaluation:** The best way to discover if the marketing practices in use are effective or not is to consistently monitor and evaluate their progress. This involves checking on the metrics and KPIs and identifying any weak areas that require modifications.

12. **Contingency plan:** The primary reason why a marketing plan can include a contingency plan is that if some unforeseeable problems suddenly occur in the course of implementing the marketing plan, the remediating procedures provided in the contingency plan can be used to bring everything under control.

13. **Conclusion:** This section summarizes all major points and facts raised in the marketing plan. Sometimes, a marketing plan's conclusion can include recommendations and other necessary information that has not been included anywhere in the plan.

14. **Appendix:** This section contains all the supplementary materials such as the outcomes of market research, financial statements, additional charts and graphics, and other documentation useful in understanding the content of the marketing plan.

Sometimes, a marketing plan may not contain all the elements described above, but it will certainly contain the most essential parts, from steps 1 to 12.

2.3 A SWOT Analysis and Its Importance

SWOT Analysis is an acronym for strengths, weaknesses, opportunities, and threats analysis. It is helpful to identify both the internal and external factors influencing an organization's operations and growth. Therefore, the insights obtained from the SWOT Analysis can be employed in crafting effective marketing strategies.

Strengths (S): Strengths are internal factors influencing the performance of an organization. They include but are not limited to a company's great reputation, possession of some sophisticated technologies, having a great team, and offering quality, competitive products/services. Organizations play to their strengths to outperform their rivals in the industry.

Weaknesses (W): Every company has its inherent weaknesses or vulnerabilities. They could be a lack of adequate funding, poor management structure, unmotivated employees, lack of culturally diverse employees, and other internally generated challenges that frustrate the company's growth or cause it to be redundant.

Opportunities (O): Opportunities are new growth avenues available to companies, which if taken, the profitability will be positively impacted. Different opportunities abound outside a company, and it takes strategic awareness of the latest industry trends, consumers' behavior, changes in marketing, product or service positioning, and knowledge of state-of-the-art technologies to take advantage of the available opportunities. This is an external factor that can determine an organization's fortune if genuine efforts are deployed toward reaching out to new consumers, partners, suppliers, etc.

Threats (T): Threats are external challenges that the company may have little control over. For example, economic policies, new governmental rules/regulations, disruption in technologies, natural disasters, powerful competitors, and so on. Good corporations normally prepare ahead for all these problems by using all the resources at their disposal to resolve whatever threats may slow down their routine operations.

Marketers usually align the outcomes of SWOT Analysis with their organization's visions to achieve planned projections. Moreover, they are expected to demonstrate a high degree of flexibility and adaptability to be able to transform their marketing initiatives.

2.3.1 Apple, Inc.: A Real-time Example of SWOT Analysis

Here we use one of the most well-known and well-understood brands as an example to perform a SWOT Analysis. Table 3.1 indicates the possible outcomes of undertaking a SWOT Analysis on Apple, Inc.

Table 2.1	SWOT Analysis for Apple, Inc.

Strengths	Weaknesses
1. **Brand reputation**: Apple, Inc., over the years, has retained its international reputation as a company that prides itself on offering high-quality products/ services. 2. **Product diversity**: The company offers a line of different products, ranging from smartphones to digital watches, computers, music, and other products. 3. **Ecosystem integration**: Apple, Inc.'s products can smoothly be integrated with one another, and they are also compatible with other non-Apple products.	1. **High price points:** Most of Apple, Inc.'s products are not for lower-middle-class consumers because they are comparatively expensive. For instance, an Apple watch costs over $250 per piece. 2. **Over-dependence on iPhones:** Apple, Inc. still hugely relies on its line of iPhones as the main source of its revenue. If any competitors come out with a line of smartphones that can technically rival Apple's iPhones, the company may find itself struggling to maintain its current level of revenue generation. 3. **Reliance on suppliers:** Till today, Apple, Inc. still depends on a number of third-party suppliers in countries such as India, China, Japan, Vietnam, Thailand, and Malaysia to produce its products. This entails that the company doesn't own its own manufacturing plants/units. If there is a sudden disruption in the supply chain, Apple may experience unexpected distribution disturbances.

Opportunities	Threats
1. **Expanding wearable market:** Apple is taking advantage of the explosive wearable market worldwide to sell its wearable devices including Apple watches.	1. **Intense competition:** Apple is facing intense competition from other tech companies that are producing the same products that it concentrates on. For example: Samsung in South Korea and Xiaomi and Huawei in China.
2. **Emerging markets:** Apple is also making inroads into some emerging markets in Africa, Asia, Latin America, etc. to market and sell its products.	2. **Supply chain disruptions:** Apple's distribution network may be affected by a sudden disruption in the global supply chain.
3. **Health and wellness technology:** Apple, Inc. has the capability to integrate its devices with other health and wellness technologies to expand its customer base.	3. **Regulatory challenges:** New regulations for tech companies may impact Apple's routine operations.

Strategic implications:

Given Apple's strategy, the following is a list of my own recommendations as to how I believe the company should set guidelines for the future.

- **Leverage brand strength:** Continue emphasizing innovation and user experience to maintain and strengthen Apple's brand reputation.

- **Address iPhone dependency:** It is imperative that Apple, Inc. diversifies its revenue source by proactively marketing its other products such as wearable devices and services.

- **Explore more emerging markets:** To drive global growth, Apple needs to invest heavily in emerging markets by reaching out to entirely new market segments that are capable of buying its products.

- **Mitigate supply chain risks:** By striking up partnerships with other suppliers, Apple can mitigate any unexpected supply chain disruption coming from its current suppliers in China, etc.

As shown in the example above, the SWOT Analysis gave Apple, Inc. the rare chance to identify its strengths, and opportunities and use those to offset threats arising from its weaknesses.

Quiz

1. **What are the components of a Marketing Plan?**

   a. The 4Ps of marketing i.e. promotion, price, people, and place

   b. Metrics, budgeting, plans, goals, and actions

   c. Opportunities, threats, strengths, weaknesses

   d. Markets, purchasing power, needs, and consumers

2. **Which principle emphasizes the segmentation of markets for targeted marketing efforts?**

   a. Understanding needs (Needs lead to market segmentation)

   b. Creation of products, services, or ideas

   c. Needs lead to markets

   d. Marketing aims to satisfy needs through 4Ps

3. **What does a SWOT analysis assess?**

   a. Market dynamics

   b. Consumer preferences

   c. Internal weakness, strengths, external opportunities, threats

   d. Marketing strategies

4. **How do strengths and weaknesses impact organizational performance?**

   a. They have no impact

   b. They influence market dynamics

   c. They impact organizational performance

   d. They affect consumer behavior

5. **Which company's example demonstrates brand reputation and ecosystem integration as strengths?**
   a. Google
   b. Microsoft
   c. Apple Inc.
   d. Samsung

6. **What does a SWOT analysis help in integrating into marketing plans?**
   a. Internal processes
   b. Market dynamics
   c. Strategic decision-making
   d. Consumer behavior

7. **Which factor poses a threat to Apple Inc. according to the example provided?**
   a. Brand reputation
   b. Ecosystem integration
   c. Intense competition
   d. Expansion into emerging markets

8. **How does the following contribute to a company's success - Increasing strengths, handling weaknesses, taking advantage of opportunities, and limiting threats?**
   a. It has no impact
   b. It optimizes strategic position for sustainable success
   c. It increases production costs
   d. It decreases market share

9. **Marketing plans function as:**

    a. Legal documents for compliance purposes

    b. Roadmaps to guide marketing activities and fuel growth

    c. Internal reports for financial analysis

    d. Product specifications for development teams

10. **Which component of a marketing plan is NOT directly involved in implementing marketing activities?**

    a. Setting success metrics

    b. Developing action plans (Action plans outline the steps to achieve goals, not direct implementation)

    c. Creating an implementation schedule

    d. Monitoring performance

Answers	1 – a	2 – c	3 – c	4 – c	5 – c
	6 – c	7 – c	8 – b	9 – b	10 – b

Chapter Summary

◆ Marketing plans are roadmaps that guide businesses through marketing activities and fuel growth.

◆ Core marketing plan components include market analysis, identification of the target audience, outlining marketing goals, developing strategy-based action plans, budgeting, designing the metrics and KPIs, setting up a workable timeline, measuring performance, evaluating the outcomes, handling unforeseeable challenges with contingency plans, and summarizing the key takeaways from the business plan.

◆ Understanding consumers is key. It is a fact that an effective marketing plan takes into consideration the consumers' spending habits, purchasing power, needs, expectations, and target markets.

◆ Needs drive innovation. Creating products/services that meet consumers' expectations requires adopting the latest technology in the market.

◆ Targeted marketing through segmentation is a crucial part of a good marketing plan. Organizations can drastically reduce their marketing budget if they are concentrating only on the right customers using the marketing mix (4P: People, Price, Place, Promotion).

◆ SWOT Analysis helps companies discover their internal strengths and weaknesses while considering the impacts of externally motivated opportunities and threats. SWOT Analysis is predominantly utilized in decision-making.

◆ Apple's SWOT Analysis reveals the following:

- **Apple's marketing strengths:** Apple survives on the strength of its brand reputation and the fact that its products/services are parts of the same ecosystem and can be integrated (compatible) with other non-Apple devices.

- **Apple's marketing weaknesses:** Apple's main weaknesses are: (i) relying only on a single product line (its iPhones), and (ii) mainly sourcing its products from overseas—an issue that can lead to supply chain disruptions.

- **Apple's marketing opportunities:** Apple has the chance to ride the ever-increasing wearable device market while growing its customer base in emerging markets.

- **Apple's marketing threats:** Apple consistently faces the risks of supply chain disruption as well as dealing with intense competition from other tech giants.

Further Reading

Refer to the following videos to enhance understanding of the concepts and examples discussed in this chapter. Links to these videos are also available in the Online Resources section of this book.

- What is marketing? https://www.youtube.com/watch?v=QusJ4fpWQwA

- 4 Ps of marketing: https://www.youtube.com/watch?v=f3L7yFPMtBw

- What is a market? https://www.youtube.com/watch?v=eNrcZ6h1Z8M

- Marketing as a process: https://www.youtube.com/watch?v=J7hLKI76ZS4

- Apple Inc. SWOT analysis: https://www.youtube.com/watch?v=jPNuiihVlC8

This page is intentionally left blank

Chapter **3**

Segmentation and Targeting Strategies: Defining Target From a Consumer Behavior Perspective

This chapter focuses on the important criteria for creating an effective marketing plan, such as having profound knowledge of the market, segmenting the target consumers, and understanding their needs/requirements. We explore the key elements that shape this process through a customer behavior lens. This chapter aims to equip readers with the knowledge and tools needed to navigate the complex terrain of market analysis, segmentation, and target audience definition, all through the lens of customer behavior.

Key learning objectives should include the reader's understanding of the following:

- Segmentation strategies
- Targeting strategies
- Positioning
- Real-life targeting case studies

3.1 Segmentation Strategies

In the vast canvas of consumer preferences, market segmentation emerges as the brushstroke that adds nuance and depth to effective marketing. This chapter starts by delving into the profound importance of segmentation, exploring its role in unraveling the intricacies of diverse consumer behaviors.

Market segmentation is the symphony that transforms a monolithic market into a nuanced composition of distinct notes.

In the 90s, Wendy's used a TV show to draw viewers' attention to a virtual country where everyone in it could only pick a single product. This was a subtle attempt by Wendy's to implore people to only focus on it and not on other companies like McDonald's and Burger King.

Wendy's was demonstrating the concept of market segmentation then. As a matter of fact, it takes careful planning and practical market research to actually identify a market segment.

A market is full of consumers with diverse behaviors, needs, interests, and preferences. However, a market segment comprises consumers with the same characteristics and tendencies. Therefore, a market segment can be created based on these four criteria:

- Demographic
- Behavioral
- Attitudinal
- Aspirational

3.1.1 Demographic segmentation

This is based on all data found on a census, so this information is easy to define and measure. People can tell you how they fit into a demographic, which is the most frequently used segmentation method. In a Census, you can retrieve the following information:

- Age
- Sex
- Race
- Address
- Civil status
- Income
- Occupation

3.1.2 Behavioral segmentation

Behavioral segmentation is all about dividing consumers into specific segments (market segments) based on their commonly shared traits or characteristics such as their actions, purchasing habits or patterns, intrinsic behaviors, and preferences in relation to goods, services, and brands. Interestingly, consumers exhibit different behaviors when it comes to their spending habits, loyalty to brands, and other attributes peculiar to a certain consumer segment.

Purchase behavior encompasses several key elements that influence consumer actions. Firstly, it includes frequency, indicating how often a consumer makes purchases within a given timeframe. Additionally, it considers volume, which refers to the quantity or amount of products purchased in a specific period. The usage pattern of a consumer reveals some useful information about their behavior. It is possible to detect their level of consumption or engagement with a product/service by analyzing their frequency of use, intensity of utilization, and depth of usage of the product/service.

Occasion-based behavior further elucidates consumer actions by considering the timing and context surrounding product usage and purchase. This includes the occasion of use, denoting when and under what circumstances consumers utilize a product or service, and the occasion of purchase, which encapsulates the events or situations triggering a purchase.

A consumer typically goes through four stages before making a purchase: First, the awareness stage—when the consumer identifies a product or service in the market that can help them solve a certain pain point; second, the consideration stage—this is when the consumer undergoes comparative research to determine the best product or service that will meet their needs; third, the decision stage—having considered the possible benefits from all the available options, this is the time for the consumer to make their final decision; and finally the purchase stage—this is when the actual transaction takes place as the consumer pays for the product or service. Lastly, post-purchase evaluation follows, wherein consumers assess their decision and overall experience with the product or service.

Organizations are usually interested in knowing the behaviors of their customers because they could be in any of the three stages in a customer lifecycle as explained below:

1. **New customers:** These customers who have just discovered the product and service and enjoy using it.

2. **Existing customers:** These include the customers who have been patronizing and utilizing the product/service for a very long time.

3. **Churned customers:** These are customers who are somehow dissatisfied with the product/service and have stopped using it.

Finally, when consumers respond to marketing communications and/or promotions, it is possible, from their tone, to detect their level of engagement or interaction with the product/service. In some positive circumstances, they could offer useful feedback on how to improve the product/service.

By leveraging behavioral segmentation, marketers can tailor their approaches to specific consumer actions, thereby enhancing targeting precision, personalizing experiences, and optimizing offerings to meet diverse consumer needs and preferences effectively.

3.1.3 Attitudinal segmentation

At times, marketers can carry out attitudinal segmentation to better know their targeted consumers with the hope of creating advertisements that will catch their attention in an obviously distracted world. In principle, attitudinal segmentation is the process of dividing consumers into a particular group or segment based on their uniquely similar attitudes, perceptions, values, beliefs, and preferences. Therefore attitudinal segmentation is a useful marketing tool that organizations take advantage of.

Critical aspects of attitudinal segmentation include:

1. **Attitudes and beliefs:**
   - Identifying consumers' attitudes toward products, brands, or specific issues
   - Understanding the underlying beliefs and values that shape their preferences

2. **Lifestyle and personality:**
   - Discovering consumers' motivations by analyzing their personality traits, lifestyles, and interests.
   - Using psychological parameters to segment consumers, and to explore how those parameters influence their choices.

3. **Perceptions and opinions:**
   - Undertaking an analysis to discover how consumers see a brand, service, or product.
   - Categorizing individuals based on their opinions about specific aspects related to the market

4. **Brand loyalty and engagement:**
   - Evaluating consumers' loyalty levels to specific brands or products
   - Assessing their engagement with brands across various touchpoints

5. Social and cultural influences:
- Considering how social and cultural factors influence consumers' attitudes
- Segmenting based on shared cultural values or affiliations with certain social groups

6. Psychological triggers:
- Recognizing the psychological triggers that influence consumer behavior
- Understanding how emotional connections and triggers impact decision-making

7. Purchase motivations:
- Analyzing the underlying motivations that drive consumers to make purchasing decisions
- Identifying whether consumers are motivated by status, convenience, value, or other factors

Attitudinal segmentation allows marketers to create effective advertising because their messages will resonate strongly with the targeted consumers whose beliefs, values, and preferences are taken into account while drafting the advertisements. This approach is precious in industries where emotional connections and brand perceptions significantly shape consumer preferences.

3.1.4 Aspirational segmentation

Aspirational segmentation, another useful marketing tactic, allows marketers to target consumers based on their individual desires, aspirations, dreams, ambitions, or the lifestyles they desire to have. This marketing strategy transcends focusing only on consumers' demographics or behaviors, it primarily concentrates on understanding and addressing the aspirations of a specific consumer segment.

There are two unique elements associated with aspirational segmentation: First, identifying consumers' aspirations, dreams, desirable lifestyles, etc. Second, creating customized marketing communications and products/services aimed at fulfilling those consumers' aspirations. Leveraging brand image and affiliation involves associating brands with the aspirational lifestyle and creating resonant brand images.

Acknowledging the importance of social recognition, marketing strategies should tap into the desire for social approval. It is imperative for organizations to develop products/services that will help consumers actualize their aspirations, ambitions, desired lifestyles, etc. More importantly, the marketing communications that they put out there must resonate with targeted consumers so as to motivate and encourage them to buy the organizations' products/ services. In this way, organizations can build long-term relationships with this consumer segment, taking into account their current needs and future requirements. This entails that organizations need to evolve over time to be able to accommodate consumers' future aspirational needs as trends change from time to time.

Industries such as fashion, travel, lifestyle products, and luxury goods are the ones mostly undertaking aspirational segmentation of their customers. They do so to be able to connect emotionally with their customers, satisfy their current and future needs, and enjoy long-term and mutually beneficial relationships with them.

3.2 Targeting Strategies

Marketers utilize "targeting" to focus their marketing efforts mostly on one or a few consumer segments. This approach is cost-effective and helps marketers to proactively deploy advertising resources toward consumers that are promising, attractive, and feasible. Instead of concentrating their advertisements on the entire market, which may be counterproductive and costly, marketers only reach out to people who can become their potential customers, and whose needs and preferences align with their organizations' goals and objectives.

Figure 3.1   **The targeting process**

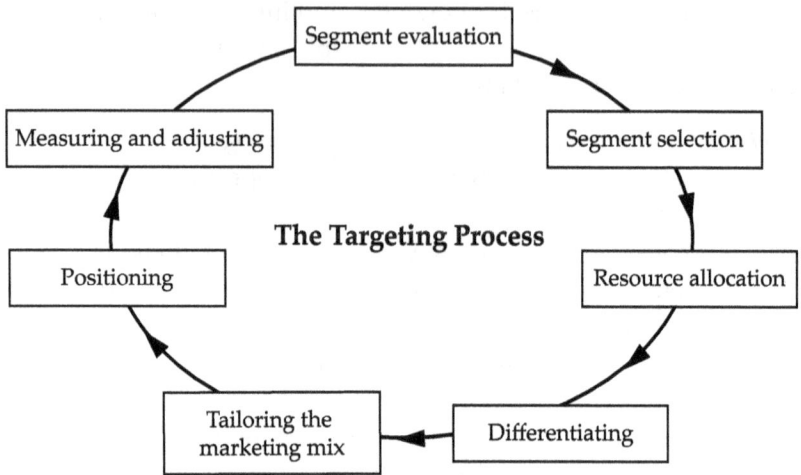

As shown in Figure 3.1, the key components of the targeting process include:

1. **Segment evaluation:**
    *   Assessing the potential of each identified segment based on factors such as size, growth potential, profitability, and compatibility with the firm's offerings
    *   Considering the competitive landscape within each segment to determine the feasibility of establishing a solid market presence

2. **Segment selection:**
    *   Choosing one or a few segments that align with the firm's overall business objectives
    *   Prioritizing segments that best fit the firm's products or services and have the most significant potential for success

3. **Resource allocation:**
    *   Allocating resources, including budget, time, and personnel, based on the selected segments

- Determining the level of investment required to reach and engage the chosen target audience effectively

4. Differentiation strategy:
- Developing a differentiation strategy to position the firm's offerings within the chosen segments uniquely
- Identifying and leveraging competitive advantages to stand out in the market

5. Tailoring the marketing mix:
- Customizing the marketing mix (product, price, place, promotion) to excite the targeted segments in relation to their needs and preferences
- Drafting marketing messages, campaigns, and positions that align with the organizational goals and are exciting to the targeted segments

6. Positioning:
- Crafting a distinct and compelling brand positioning within the minds of the target consumers
- Communicating the firm's unique value proposition to the selected segments

7. Measuring and adjusting:
- Implementing metrics to measure the success of the targeting strategy
- Consistently assessing market dynamics to ensure that it is in tandem with consumer behavior. If there are issues, it is advisable to make some necessary adjustments

The two important outcomes of successful consumer targeting are that it gives an organization the opportunity to clearly understand its customers' problems so as to provide products/services that will solve their pain points. Moreover, taking good care of consumers can foster a strong relationship between them and the organization, thereby turning the consumers into loyal customers who will patronize the organization's products/services for a very long time.

3.3 Positioning

Positioning can be defined as a marketing strategy whereby marketers utilize understandable visuals and brand identity to create vivid imagery about a product/service in the minds of consumers. This helps consumers to be able to quickly identify that product/service in the marketplace, among others. Consumers can easily choose the product/services having been fully aware of its benefits and can easily differentiate it from the other products/services.

For example, McDonald's is positioned as a family restaurant that whets the appetites of families, most especially their children. So, consumers clearly understand the message/positioning, and this is why many parents believe that McDonald's is where they should often take their children.

Critical elements of positioning include:

1. **Differentiation:**
   - Identifying and communicating unique features, benefits, or attributes that set the brand apart
   - Highlighting what makes the product or service superior or distinct in the eyes of consumers

2. **Target audience:**
   - Having a good understanding of consumers' aspirations, needs, and preferences
   - Customizing the positioning message to be compatible with the target consumer segment (s)

3. **Value proposition:**

- Clearly articulating the value proposition[1] that the brand promises to deliver
- Communicating how the product or service addresses a particular problem or fulfills a specific need better than alternatives

4. **Consistency:**

- Ensuring consistency in messaging across all marketing channels
- Aligning every aspect of the brand's communication to reinforce the desired positioning

5. **Competitive context:**

- Discovering the opportunities for differentiation in the competitive market landscape.
- Positioning the product/service/brand in a way that is memorable, distinct, and identifiable in the market.

6. **Emotional connection:**

- By appealing to consumers' preferences and values, it is possible to connect them emotionally to the products/services
- Developing a brand identity or personality that matches consumers' aspirations or desires

7. **Long-term perspective:**

- Developing a positioning strategy with a long-term perspective
- The positioning evolves as the market and consumer preferences change over time

---

1 A value proposition is a concise statement that summarizes why a customer should choose your product or service. It communicates the clear benefit that a customer receives. It's essentially an explanation of how your offering solves a specific problem or fulfills a need for the customer, differentiating you from competitors.

3.3.1 Positioning statement:

A positioning statement is usually a single-sentence, concise, and direct marketing communication that highlights a product's/service's unique valuable proposition and its comparative position in the market. It serves as a means of informing consumers about how an organization wants them to perceive and use its product/service, thereby benefiting from using it.

Some critical components of a positioning statement include:

1. **Target audience:** Clearly defining the primary audience for the product or brand

2. **Frame of reference:** Describing the category or market in which the brand operates

3. **Unique value proposition:** Articulating the unique benefits or attributes that differentiate the brand from competitors

4. **Reasons to believe:** Providing evidence or reasons that support the brand's claim of superiority

5. **Brand personality:** Revealing the true brand personality or character to consumers.

6. **Desired consumer perception:** Describing the kind of perception the organization wants consumers to have about its brand.

A well-prepared positioning statement won't only help the organization achieve its marketing goals, but it will also present an image of consistency and viability to the organization's customers-these two desirable attributes that will keep the organization's customers glued to the products/services.

3.4 Real-Life Targeting Cases

When done properly and conscientiously, targeting and positioning can suddenly bring an obscure company into the limelight to compete with well-known brands. There are some recent examples to support this assertion. Before they became household names, companies like Hyundai, Oakley, and Dove were totally unknown. This case study revealed what they did exactly and how such an action made them popular within a few years.

1. **Targeting and segmentation - Oakley:**[2]

   - **Targeting:** From its beginning, Oakley has focused primarily on providing eyewear to athletes and supporters of outdoor activities, especially the cycling community. Over the years though, it has expanded its market base making eyewear for other sport enthusiasts.

   - **Segmentation:** By specializing in sports such as skiing, cycling, and golf, Oakley has already segmented its market base.

2. **Positioning ingenuity - Hyundai:**[3]

   - **Positioning:** Hyundai caught the attention of consumers when it positioned itself as a dependable and affordable automobile in a market full of expensive vehicles. The brand's budget-friendly reputation is compatible with its quality and innovation.

   - **Differentiation:** Hyundai differentiates itself through features and technology. Models like the Sonata and

---

2 Jabin. "Oakley: How the Eyewear Giant Drives Growth and Captures Its Market." *The MarTech Summit* (blog), January 12, 2024. https://themartechsummit.com/oakley-influencer-marketing/.

3 TBH, Team. "Marketing Strategies, Marketing Mix & STP of Hyundai." The Brand Hopper, September 2, 2023. https://thebrandhopper.com

Elantra emphasize advanced safety and connectivity options.

3. Adaptability and market evolution - Dove's evolution

- **Targeting:** Dove evolved its targeting by expanding beyond women to men. The "Real Beauty" concept went beyond challenging stereotypes and establishing beauty standards for all.

- **Positioning:** Dove has become a force to be reckoned with in the cosmetics industry because it promotes body positivity and self-esteem.

The triumphs of Dove, Oakley, and Hyundai underscore that market mastery is not exclusive to industry giants. Through thoughtful targeting and strategic positioning, these brands have woven success stories that resonate with specific audiences, proving that even in the shadows, market brilliance can shine brightly.

Quiz

1. **Which of the following statements is a primary benefit of segmentation in marketing?**
   a. Increasing production costs
   b. Limiting market reach
   c. Offering a nuanced understanding of diverse consumer behaviors
   d. Decreasing customer satisfaction

2. **Which of these is NOT a segmentation type?**
   a. Demographic
   b. Geographic
   c. Behavioral
   d. Attitudinal

3. **What does the targeting process involve?**
   a. Creating brand awareness
   b. Conducting market research
   c. Segment evaluation, selection, and resource allocation
   d. Developing new products

4. **What is positioning in marketing?**
   a. Setting product prices
   b. Creating a distinct image and identity for a brand
   c. Choosing distribution channels
   d. Conducting competitor analysis

5. **Which segmentation dimension focuses on beliefs, values, and opinions?**

   a. Demographic

   b. Geographic

   c. Attitudinal

   d. Behavioral

6. **What is the significance of aspirational segmentation?**

   a. Capturing consumers' basic demographic information

   b. Identifying consumers' past purchasing behaviors

   c. Capturing consumers' desires and lifestyle aspirations

   d. Analyzing consumers' geographic locations

7. **How does the targeting process contribute to marketing success?**

   a. By limiting market reach

   b. By increasing production costs

   c. By enabling firms to focus on promising opportunities

   d. By reducing customer engagement

8. **Evaluating segments during the targeting process involves assessing their**

   a. Brand awareness levels only

   b. Size, growth potential, and compatibility with company objectives

   c. Geographic location solely

   d. Predominant social media platforms used

9. **Allocating resources during targeting involves**

   a. Dividing the marketing budget equally among all segments

   b. Prioritizing resources towards the most promising segments

   c. Focusing resources solely on online marketing channels

   d. Investing heavily in traditional advertising

10. **The marketing mix (4Ps) refers to**

    a. Product features, pricing models, distribution channels, and sales techniques

    b. Market research methodologies, brand positioning strategies, and competitor analysis tools

    c. Customer service experiences, loyalty programs, and social media engagement metrics

    d. Product development lifecycles, production costs, and distribution channels

Answers	1 – c	2 – d	3 – c	4 – b	5 – c
	6 – c	7 – c	8 – b	9 – b	10 – a

Chapter Summary

◆ Organizations have a lot to gain from undertaking market segmentation because it offers them a rare peek into consumers' behaviors, aspirations, attitudes, and demographics.

◆ Practically, it is possible to segment a market based on demographics such as age, location, and income. Behavioral segmentation is all about understanding the logic behind consumers' buying patterns, brand loyalty, and their occasional actions. Attitudinal segmentation mainly concentrates on consumers' values, beliefs, and perceptions, while aspirational segmentation focuses on consumers' desires, lifestyle aspirations, and behavior.

◆ Targeting involves several steps. First, we evaluate and select segments. Then, we allocate resources, differentiate our offerings, and tailor the marketing mix (4Ps) to each segment. Finally, we develop a unique positioning strategy and continuously measure its effectiveness.

◆ Targeting makes it possible for firms to concentrate on profitable market segments in order to maximize their resource utilization, and build lasting relationships with their customers.

◆ Positioning is an important concept that allows organizations to create vivid imagery and identity for a brand in the minds of consumers.

◆ The elements of effective positioning include differentiation, knowing the target audience, presenting a convincing value proposition, establishing consistency across messaging, putting the organization's competitive edge in the context, and creating an emotional connection with consumers.

◆ It should be noted that great positioning streamlines marketing efforts by releasing clear and consistent brand messages.

◆ Brands like Dove (empowering women), Oakley (performance for athletes), and Hyundai (value-driven cars for families) strategically navigate the market by understanding target audience needs, carving distinct niches, and aligning offerings with evolving consumer preferences.

◆ The above-mentioned examples pinpointed the significance and impact of targeting and positioning.

◆ By understanding the different types of consumers, segmenting them in a strategic manner, and creating distinct and memorable brand positioning, companies can successfully reach their desired audience without actually breaking the bank.

Further Reading

Refer to the following videos to enhance understanding of the concepts and examples discussed in this chapter. Links to these videos are also available in the Online Resources section of this book.

- Wendy's single market, no segment strategy commercial: https://www.youtube.com/watch?v=5CaMUfxVJVQ

- Market segmentation: https://www.youtube.com/watch?v=hnz1kClvHcs

- Targeting strategy: https://www.youtube.com/watch?v=iGOw39GWDaI

- Hyundai marketing strategy: https://www.youtube.com/watch?v=JHWLSSl-CFc

- Oakley marketing strategy: https://www.youtube.com/watch?v=tL7zcd2fXCk

- Specialized marketing strategy: https://www.youtube.com/watch?v=OtwYIFKLbuQ

- Dove marketing strategy: https://www.youtube.com/watch?v=GirRXvVUR28

Chapter **4**

Psychological Issues: What Motivates Consumers

Chapter four reviews psychological issues related to consumer behavior, delving into the intricate realm of human motivations. From Maslow's hierarchy of needs to contemporary theories and emotional insights, this chapter explores the underlying drivers that shape consumer decisions. It examines how marketers can leverage these insights to segment target audiences effectively and craft compelling marketing strategies aligned with consumer motivations.

Key learning objectives should include the reader's understanding of the following:

- Unveiling the complex landscape of human motivations and its impact on consumer behavior
- Foundations of motivation, basic human needs, and Freudian theory
- Contemporary motivational theories
- Emotional influences on motivation
- Motivational applications in marketing

4.1 Consumer Behavior in Marketing: What Motivates Consumers

Embarking on exploring consumer behavior unveils a dynamic and intricate landscape shaped by human motivations. Understanding these motivations is not just a psychological endeavor; it's a strategic imperative for any savvy marketer.

At its core, consumer behavior is intricately linked to fundamental human needs. The psychological tapestry is rich and nuanced, from Maslow's hierarchy influencing purchasing decisions to Freudian desires shaping brand preferences. In our contemporary marketing landscape, theories like Herzberg's two-factor, self-determination, and expectancy-value guide us in deciphering the intricate dance of consumer motivations.

Yet, the heartbeat of consumer behavior lies in emotions.

The useful insights garnered from psychology and neuroscience confirm that consumers often respond to both positive and negative triggers. This knowledge of their emotional responses can be used to have some influence on their brains and, to a large extent, on their decision-making and buying patterns.

Therefore, a marketing manager needs to utilize these insights, in a good way, to create marketing materials or promotional content that can resonate with the emotions of their target audience/customer segment.

This chapter explores how ideas obtained from psychology and neuroscience can offer practical techniques marketers can utilize to better understand the underlying motivation prompting their customers to act favorably toward their organizations' products/services.

4.2 Foundations of Motivation

4.2.1 Maslow's hierarchy of needs

When considering the most practical framework for understanding consumers' psychological motivation, Abraham Maslow's hierarchy of needs is of great importance. As shown in Figure 4.1, at the bottom of the pyramid are human's basic needs, such as warmth, food, rest, and water. At the pinnacle of the pyramid lies human's self-fulfillment needs, like self-actualization or fulfilling one's potential.

In consumer behavior, Maslow's theory underscores that purchasing decisions often align with satisfying these hierarchical needs. Whether seeking essentials like food and shelter or striving for self-actualization through premium products, understanding where consumers fall on this pyramid is vital to effective marketing strategies.

Figure 4.1 **Maslow's hierarchy of needs**

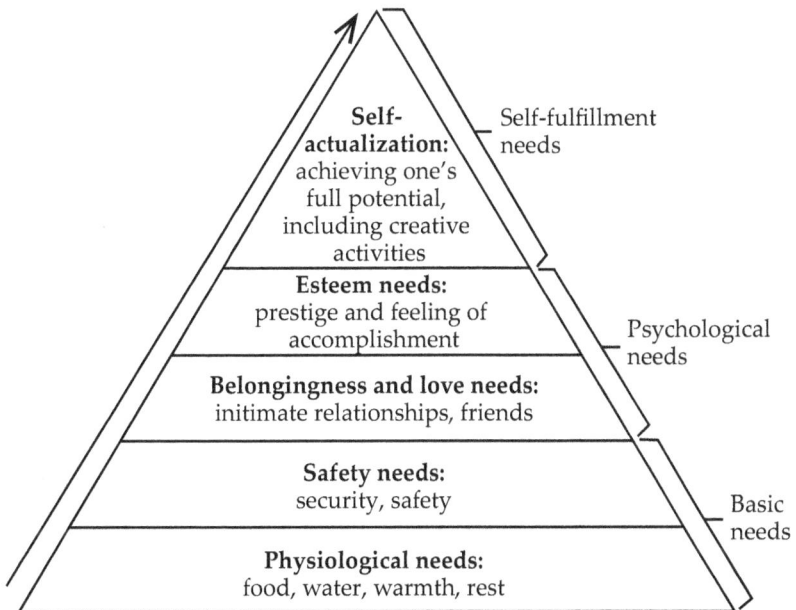

Source: https://www.projectmaslow.org/maslows-hierarchy-of-needs/

Each of Maslov's needs is analyzed below:

1. **Physical needs:** The bottom of the pyramid represents a human's basic needs, which include food, warmth, water, air, shelter, etc. They are the fundamental requirements that everyone needs for survival.

2. **Safety needs:** Safety needs illustrate elements related to security and safety. This might include a home, employment, health, and stability.

3. **Love and belongingness:** In the middle of the pyramid, these needs depict relationships, friendships, and a sense of belonging.

4. **Esteem needs:** Above love and belongingness, it draws symbols of achievement, recognition, and self-worth. This might include images of awards, success, or individuals expressing confidence.

5. **Self-actualization needs:** These needs are at the pyramid's top, and they are about human's intense desire to achieve their potential in life or actualize their personal goals and ambitions.

Astute marketers understand that Maslov's hierarchy of needs is not only a psychological concept, but also a powerful marketing tool they can utilize in their marketing strategies. Having a deep knowledge of consumers' primary needs can equip marketers with the right amount of information they can use to deploy targeted promotions or marketing towards them.

Highlighted below are some examples of campaigns that incorporated some aspects of Maslov's psychology of motivation:

1. **Targeted messaging: Nike's "Just Do It" campaign**

    Nike's famous campaign's slogan plays to consumers' **self-actualization** agenda. Encouraging them to act proactively shows that they (the consumers) feel motivated by Nike's motivational message which pushes them to fearlessly pursue their dreams and score significant achievements in their lives. It is indeed a powerful message that is still boosting consumers' self-esteem.

2. **Product positioning: Whole Foods Market**

By emphasizing that its products are high-quality and organic, Whole Foods positioned itself as a business that concerns itself with its customers' safety and well-being. Consumers like the brand because they believe it caters for their health and self-esteem. Without a doubt, Whole Foods meets the consumers' **safety needs** and self-protection goals.

3. **Creating emotional connections: Coca-Cola's "Share a Coke" campaign**

With this campaign, Coca-Cola tapped into consumers' emotional connections and bonds. Allowing consumers to personally share love, writing the names of their loved ones on Coke bottles, and sharing the drinks with them fulfilled Maslov's hierarchy of **love and belongingness.**

4. **Segmentation and targeting: Apple's market segmentation**

Apple effectively targets different consumer segments. The iPhone caters to **esteem and self-actualization needs**, positioning itself as an innovative and aspirational product. Simultaneously, more affordable products like the iPad meet **safety and belongingness needs**, expanding the brand's reach.

5. **Brand loyalty: Starbucks' loyalty program**

Starbucks' loyalty program offers discounts (addressing **financial needs**) and provides a sense of **belonging**. Exclusive offers and personalized rewards contribute to customers' esteem, fostering loyalty beyond mere transactions.

6. **Product development: Fitbit fitness trackers**

Fitbit's product development aligns with various levels of the hierarchy. By promoting a healthy lifestyle, the consumers' **physiological needs** are properly taken care of.

Similarly, encouraging consumers to monitor their health parameters has equally met their **safety needs,** and their **self-esteem needs** are fulfilled by offering the much-needed advice that they should do everything within their power to achieve their fitness goals.

In conclusion, Maslov's hierarchy of needs equips marketers with some practical advice they require in order to design effective marketing strategies and products that consumers will like and patronize. By understanding and incorporating these principles, brands can forge lasting connections and meet diverse consumer motivations.

4.3 Freudian Theory and Its Application to Marketing

Sigmund Freud is considered the father of psychoanalysis, and his immense contributions in this field have shed more light on how human behaviors are influenced by their subconscious minds. His Freudian Theory has been regarded as a profound psychological framework, and it clearly describes the three main components of the human psyche, namely: the id, ego, and superego. Postulated in 1923, his theory was named "The Ego and the Id", and it is also referred to as "Das Ich und das Es," in German.

The id symbolizes the highest and most spontaneous aspect of the human mind which, against all societal norms and trends, seeks to attain a state of maximum pleasure and gratification. The primary goals of the id are to pursue personal desires and basic needs. The id operates at the subconscious level and drives impulses and irrational behaviors.

The ego mediates among the id's impulses, the superego's moralistic principles, and the world at large. The ego functions sensibly, trying to fulfill the id's desires in a more acceptable way. Interestingly, the ego aims to maintain a psychological balance by holding the id's impulsive desires under the constraints of the superego's moral standards.

The superego expresses societal norms and moralistic principles, operating as the conscience. It uses feelings of shame, guilt, or pride to enforce compliance with societal norms and ethical requirements. Since the superego constantly functions as the promoter of moral integrity, it always clashes with the id, which operates with little or no societal value.

Within the human psyche, the three above-mentioned components interact dynamically in a way that personal behaviors and personality development are shaped. The Freudian Theory opens a new perspective for understanding the psychological motivation behind human behaviors.

4.3.1 Applying Freudian theory to marketing

The Freudian Theory introduces marketers to the underlying psychological factors influencing consumers' behaviors. Understanding that symbols, emotions, and desires play a significant role in how a consumer behaves, marketers have learned to employ specific symbolism, targeted messaging, and imagery to subconsciously influence consumers' buying decisions and patterns.

The Freudian Theory offers marketers a lens into understanding human's subconscious minds, and how consumers' choices or preferences are based on a number of internal motivations. To target consumers with marketing messages that will spur an emotional connection to a brand and its products/ services, marketers need to apply their knowledge of Freudian Theory in their marketing strategies.

Outlined below are some real-life examples of how the Freudian Theory can be applied in marketing efforts:

1. **Symbolic imagery: Jaguar's "Alive" campaign**

   By employing Freudian symbols in this campaign, Jaguar taps into consumers' subconscious desires for prestige, status, and recognition for owning and driving a luxury car.

2. **Sensory appeal: Chanel's fragrance marketing**

As a world-famous manufacturer of cosmopolitan fragrances, Chanel utilized Freudian concepts to entice consumers with products that play to their taste for self-gratification and luxury. Users of Chanel's fragrances may believe they are sophisticated, and that could boost their self-esteem.

3. **Emotional resonance: Dove's "Real Beauty" campaign**

Dove's campaign aims at redefining beauty in a way that consumers can experience a great deal of self-acceptance and self-importance. The campaign used the elements of Freudian ideas that emphasize the emotional connection to personal beauty and well-being.

4. **Impulse buying triggers: Snickers' "You're Not You When You're Hungry"**

Snickers employs Freudian concepts humorously. Their campaign suggests that hunger alters one's personality, playing on the subconscious desire for emotional stability. The message triggers impulse buying by addressing immediate emotional needs.

The above-mentioned marketing examples reveal how shrewd marketers can apply Freudian principles in their marketing activities to better connect emotionally and creatively with their target market segments in order to influence their decision-making processes.

4.4 Contemporary Motivational Theories

To better understand the psychological motivations behind consumers' decision-making, it may be helpful to explore three more theories, namely, Herzberg's two-factor theory, expectancy-value theory, and self-determination theory.

4.4.1 Herzberg's two-factor theory

This theory proposes two primary factors influencing job satisfaction and dissatisfaction: hygiene factors and motivators. The hygiene factors consist of factors like the working conditions, while motivators are directly linked to the job, such as personal achievements. If Herzberg's two-factor theory is applied to consumer satisfaction, it can be translated in this form: hygiene factors indicate initial expectations, while motivators boost the experience. For example, if a patient visits a hospital, the hygiene factors could be a clean facility (hospital room), while the motivators could be personalized clinical service that will increase healthcare delivery satisfaction.

4.4.2 Self-determination theory (SDT)

This theory states that self-determination is activated by some essential factors like competence, relatedness, and autonomy. Therefore, in consumerism, competence is all about mastering the diverse consumer experiences; autonomy refers to enjoying the freedom one has in making decisions or choices that align with one's personal needs; and relatedness emphasizes creating connections between brands and consumers based on the latter's individual values and preferences. Apple, Inc., for example, displays self-determination theory in action when it manufactures products that can be customized by users in accordance with their needs (autonomy), with a seamless design (competence), and filling every user with the feeling of belonging to the Apple family (relatedness).

4.4.3 Expectant-value theory

This theory explains that consumers make a choice to purchase a product based on the expected outcomes and their intrinsic values. For example, when a person is buying a laptop, the expected outcome may be that the product will be durable.

Therefore, the intrinsic value of the laptop is linked to its durability.

As a matter of fact, Herzberg's theory defines the dual conditions for satisfaction; the SDT highlights the inherent motivators; and the expectancy-value theory describes the factors leading to consumers' decision-making. Skillful marketers can incorporate great ideas from these three, above-stated theories into their marketing strategies to better understand how consumers' expression of satisfaction can motivate them in making buying decisions.

The following examples demonstrate how the three theories mentioned above can be applied to marketing:

1. For a company like Peloton, consumers' autonomy is revealed by empowering them to customize their workouts; by taking routine classes and being evaluated thereafter to ascertain performance, users exude a sense of achievement if they are doing well; virtual and social networking fill the users with a feeling of relatedness, as they pursue a common goal of achieving a better lifestyle.

2. In the case of Netflix, consumers expected that they would be able to access a large amount of on-demand streaming content provided by the company, based on their entertainment needs. They value the variety and rich content provided by Netflix, and the step taken by the company to offer content as premium content without ads fulfills their individual expectations.

4.5 Emotional Influences on Motivation

Human emotions are so powerful and, on most occasions, serve as motivations for making strategic decisions. Normally, emotions shape individuals' goals, desires, priorities, and, of course, actions. There are various theories and frameworks that explain how human emotions are the driving forces behind their decision-making processes.

4.5.1 Affective Events Theory (AET)

The Affective Events Theory (AET) states that a person's emotional experiences at the workplace have either a negative or positive impact on their motivation. Emotions that are classified as positive, such as pride or joy in one's work can result in positive workplace motivation. On the other hand, negative emotions like frustration and anger may cause someone to lose motivation at work, and this experience can equally have a negative effect on their wellbeing.

4.5.2 Emotion Regulation Theory

This theory describes the practice of regulating one's emotions. It is believed that those who can effectively regulate their emotions can easily achieve a specific goal. The purpose of this theory is that individual emotional regulation can reduce emotional stress, enhance motivation, and lead to goal-oriented behavior. By undertaking a positive evaluation of a past, stressful event, someone can devise the most strategic approach to deal decisively with a similar event in the future, while proactively managing their feelings or emotions.

4.5.3 Self-determination Theory (SDT)

This theory confirms that emotions play a significant role in motivation, most especially when linked to autonomy, competence, and relatedness. A person may experience a positive emotion when they identify competence, feel connected, and have the opportunity to exercise their own power of autonomy in decision-making.

4.5.4 Expectancy-value theory

The expectancy-value theory posits that emotional motivation may be connected to certain outcomes and their perceived values.

People naturally pursue a goal that will produce a desirable outcome based on its inherent value. Positive emotions like happiness and excitement about an activity can cause its value to be appreciated in the minds of those engaged in it because they are actually happy doing it. On the other hand, negative emotions such as fear or disappointment can reduce the perceived value of an event if those participating in it are no longer deriving any pleasure from it.

4.5.5 Mood-congruent motivation

This explains the obvious that people's actions are mainly motivated by their current emotional states. For example, a happy person may be open to exploring more exciting activities that can add more value to their current state of happiness. On the other hand, a tired person may choose to avoid unpleasant events that can cause them to become more tired, irrespective of the benefits attached to such events.

As a matter of fact, organizations have a lot to gain by paying attention to how consumers' emotions motivate and influence their actions and decision-making. By applying this knowledge, it will be possible to promote positive emotional responses, transform well-being, and foster interpersonal motivations.

The following are a few examples of emotional motivations in consumer behavior.

1. **Airbnb:**

   Airbnb explores the emotional connection between traveling and creating remarkable experiences that will last long in one's memories. Therefore, each time guests stay at a designated Airbnb facility, they are reminded to foster a robust relationship with their hosts, culturally and otherwise to be able to have a memorable stay with their hosts.

2. **Disney:**

   Disney often utilizes neuroscientific principles in its storytelling by weaving narratives that can cause emotionally charged responses from consumers and equally encourage them to take action immediately. This might account for why many kids love Disney and its admirable characters. Disney's theme parks incorporate neuroscientific ideas in their designs and primarily focus on building sensory and emotional connection, invoking a magical feeling that often results in out-of-this-world consumer experiences.

3. **NeuroLeap (Neuroscience in marketing):**

   As a marketing strategy, NeuroLeap employs neuroscience to analyze consumers' responses to advertisements. By paying attention to how consumers' brains work, companies can detect the emotional triggers in them and create promotional materials that can initiate positive emotions and motivations in consumers so that they can have favorable dispensation to the companies' products/services.

The examples provided above illustrate how organizations can take advantage of neuroscience to influence consumers' behaviors through emotional connections.

4.6 Consumer Segmentation Based on Motivations

As demonstrated in this chapter with some applicable examples, it is clear that consumers' behaviors are shaped or influenced by some internal motivations, which are essentially emotional or psychological motivators. This realization can equip marketers with the appropriate knowledge or insights they need to customize their marketing messaging in a way that can resonate with their target consumer segments and invoke favorable responses. When consumers are motivated emotionally, they can subconsciously make buying or purchasing decisions in favor of the advertisers.

When targeting fitness enthusiasts, a company can highlight how the great technology of their sports shoes can help them enhance their performance. Similarly, fashionistas want to know how a particular fashion can make them look great or more beautiful. This is why it is helpful to emphasize a product's/service's usefulness in a way that resonates with users emotionally.

Knowing "why" consumers need certain products can help marketers customize their positioning messages and effectively connect with them.

The following are two examples of motivational segmentation aimed at consumers within specific market segments:

1. **Value-seekers:** This market segment wants the best value for their money. They want products/services that are gratifying, durable, and highly useful. They may equally be attracted to brands offering discounts, affordable products, or loyalty programs. When marketing to this category of people, it is advisable to focus on the qualities of the products/services that compensate users or consumers for their money.

2. **Status-seekers:** This consumer segment's primary goal is to be associated with a brand image/reputation and derive some recognition from using the brand's products/services. Consumers who patronize high-end luxury products, high-label fashions, and products already endorsed by celebrities and famous people. To effectively market to these categories of consumers, it is sensible to highlight the prestige, luxury, and exclusivity of the products/services.

Example 1: Fitbit

Motivations: Wellness and Health

Segmentation strategy: Products/services such as heart rate monitoring, fitness challenges, and sleep tracking excite wellness and health-conscious enthusiasts, and that is the reason why they subscribed to Fitbit.

Example 2: HelloFresh

Motivations: Convenience and Culinary Interest

Segmentation Strategy: What HelloFresh offers consumers who are conscious about healthy eating are ingredients and recipes that are already pre-portioned. Having the convenience to prepare whatever meals they desire on time causes HelloFresh customers to stick with the company.

Example 3: Apple, Inc.

Motivations: Status and innovation

Segmentation strategy: Apple, Inc. goes after the consumer segment that perceives its sleek and high-performance products as a status symbol. Apple, Inc. emphasizes in its advertising as a company that is doing things differently, with cutting-edge technology.

Example 4: Airbnb

Motivations: Experience and Exploration

Marketing Strategy: Airbnb's marketing revolves around unique travel experiences. Through captivating storytelling and user-generated content, they appeal to individuals motivated by the desire for memorable and culturally rich journeys.

These examples showcase how companies strategically employ motivational insights to understand their target audience, resulting in effective segmentation and marketing strategies.

4.7 Applying Motivational Concepts to Your Business

Let's imagine you have to market a new car, a pair of jeans, or a cellular phone. We are going to create an imaginary exercise where we will apply motivational concepts to your marketing plan. This exercise applies to all products, services, or ideas. We will add these new, radical concepts to our business. The art of strategic positioning unfolds as we delve into behavioral and attitudinal concepts, recognizing their power to etch lasting imprints in the consumer psyche.

In crafting a narrative for new jeans, profitability can be achieved through a positioning that transcends mere functionality. Jeans poised as both fancy and correctly priced are likely to carve a deeper niche in consumers' minds, setting them apart from their counterparts positioned solely on price. This exercise emphasizes that perceived value, often rooted in aspirational and emotional connections, can be a potent driver for consumers willing to invest in more than just a commodity.

The exercise extends to marketing a new car, where the aspirational aspects play a pivotal role. The challenge lies in aligning the car's positioning with consumer aspirations, ensuring that the product meets and surpasses expectations. Strategic differentiation from competitors is essential, creating a unique space that resonates with the target audience. Again, a car that is sold to consumers for its durability and style will beat a car positioned only, in marketing, as a nice car to drive around. Consumers will surely want to spend their money on cars that can last for many years.

As a ubiquitous yet highly competitive product, the cellular phone demands a nuanced approach. Strategic positioning should consider functional attributes and delve into the emotional and aspirational realms. The exercise encourages marketers to explore ways a cellular phone can be positioned as more than a device, possibly as a lifestyle or status symbol. A real-world example is Xiaomi partnering with Leica for their top-of-the-line phones. This co-branding brings Leica´s excellent positioning to a brand that is doing its best to reach consumers in the Western world.

This holistic perspective underscores the reality check – a reminder that effective marketing goes beyond perception. The product must substantiate the promises made through its positioning, fostering customer satisfaction and safeguarding brand credibility.

In essence, this exercise demonstrates that the fusion of psychological insights into marketing strategies contributes not only to brand appeal but also to increased profitability, competitive differentiation, and sustained customer loyalty.

Refer to the Online Resources section of the book on www.vibrantpublishers.com to access more practical hands-on exercises on motivation and consumer behavior.

Quiz

1. **Why is understanding human motivations crucial for marketers?**

   a. Craft messages that resonate with consumer desires and needs

   b. Predict what products and services will be most successful

   c. Tailor marketing campaigns to specific customer segments

   d. Develop pricing strategies that align with consumer value perceptions

2. **What theory emphasizes the role of emotions in shaping consumer decisions?**

   a. Maslow's Hierarchy of Needs

   b. Affective Events Theory

   c. The Two-Factor Theory

   d. Self-Determination Theory

3. **How can marketers leverage Freudian Theory in their strategies?**

   a. Focus on product functionality and practicality

   b. Appeal to consumers' sense of logic and reason

   c. Use symbolic imagery and emotional associations to connect with subconscious desires

   d. Directly promote products based on their technical specifications

4. **According to Herzberg's Two-Factor Theory, what motivates employees to perform well?**

   a. Job security and basic benefits

   b. Recognition, achievement, and growth opportunities

   c. A combination of both hygiene and motivator factors

   d. Salary and compensation alone

5. **Which motivational theory explains how consumers choose options based on expected value?**

   a. Self-Determination Theory

   b. Expectancy-Value Theory

   c. Freudian Theory

   d. Affective Events Theory

6. **How does Fitbit's marketing strategy target a specific consumer segment?**

   a. Focus on the latest technological advancements in fitness trackers

   b. Appeal to consumers seeking a healthy lifestyle (wellness)

   c. Showcase the product's sleek and stylish design

   d. Emphasize its affordability compared to competitors

7. **Why is strategic positioning crucial for products like jeans?**

   a. Ensure efficient distribution to retail stores

   b. Create a compelling narrative around the brand and product, differentiating it from competitors

   c. Set a competitive price point for the product

   d. Highlight the technical features and materials used in the jeans

8. **Why is strategic positioning crucial for products like jeans, cars, and phones?**

    a. To offer the lowest price in the market

    b. To connect with consumer aspirations and emotional connections

    c. To provide detailed technical specifications

    d. To simplify the manufacturing process

9. **What is the main takeaway from the example of Xiaomi's partnership with Leica?**

    a. Focus on reducing production costs

    b. Strategic partnerships can enhance brand perception

    c. Price wars are essential for market share

    d. Extensive advertising is key to success

10. **Beyond psychology, what other factors influence consumer behavior?**

    a. Marketing strategies only

    b. Social and cultural influences

    c. Product features alone

    d. Brand name recognition solely

Answers	1 – a	2 – b	3 – c	4 – b	5 – b
	6 – b	7 – b	8 – b	9 – b	10 – b

Chapter Summary

◆ Psychological principles are fundamental to understanding consumer behavior.

◆ Motivation theories like Maslow's Hierarchy and Self-Determination Theory provide insights into what drives people to buy.

◆ Emotions significantly impact decision-making, with both positive and negative feelings influencing choices.

◆ Building emotional connections with consumers strengthens brand loyalty.

◆ Freudian concepts explore unconscious desires and their application in marketing strategies (symbols, brand persona, emotional appeals).

◆ Modern theories like Herzberg's Two-Factor and Expectancy-Value Theory delve into intrinsic motivations and decision-making based on expected outcomes.

◆ Motivation-based segmentation allows brands to target consumers based on specific desires (wellness, convenience, innovation, etc.).

◆ Understanding consumer psychology helps businesses create strategic positioning, compelling narratives, and marketing campaigns that resonate with their target audience.

Further Reading

Refer to the following videos to enhance understanding of the concepts and examples discussed in this chapter. Links to these videos are also available in the Online Resources section of this book.

- Nike's Just Do It Campaign: https://www.youtube.com/watch?v=TRAGvw8R0DE

- Starbucks loyalty case: https://www.youtube.com/watch?v=dmxVlSuFDvw

- Fitbit marketing case: https://www.youtube.com/watch?v=Y8trpViOm-U

- Jaguar Alive ads: https://www.youtube.com/watch?v=x5kCfXIPcfw

- Snicker ads: https://www.youtube.com/watch?v=GP6XG-s32y8

- Spotify marketing case: https://www.youtube.com/watch?v=E878NrDqdiA

- Peloton marketing case: https://www.youtube.com/watch?v=4jNypIQWzN0

- Netflix marketing case: https://www.youtube.com/watch?v=J1_zLre6wIQ

- Airbnb marketing case: https://www.youtube.com/watch?v=WzGhFmiB9G0

- Neuromarketing: https://www.youtube.com/watch?v=mkDVC_izIV0

- Hello Fresh CEO interview: https://www.youtube.com/watch?v=RibPAaPqkyo

Chapter **5**

Social Evolution: Exploring the 'Jones Effect' and Our Persistent Social Structures

Chapter five will evaluate the intricate tapestry of consumer behavior with respect to social dynamics. This chapter echoes the age-old adage that humans are inherently social beings and that social dynamics play a pivotal role in consumer behavior. It delves into the profound influence of our evolutionary roots on contemporary consumer behaviors, exploring the persistence of communal instincts and the omnipresent "Jones Effect."

Key learning objectives should include the reader's understanding of the following:

- Consumer behavior analysis based on initial human behaviors
- Tribal mentality
- The "Jones Effect"
- Social media and the digital tribe

5.1 Tribal Mentality

In the vast landscape of consumer behavior, the concept of tribes extends far beyond traditional anthropological contexts. Professor Robert Dewar's insights on modern humans continuing to live in tribes find resonance in brand loyalty.[4] This chapter explores the phenomenon of cult-like followings for specific brands akin to old tribes, where unique languages, symbols, heroes, ceremonies, and identifications create a sense of belonging. I would dare to state that speaking about "marketing tribes" is probably the most relevant concept you will find in this book and it is yet to be totally and formally developed in the marketing world.

Here, we delve into five examples exemplifying the powerful connection between brands and their devoted tribes.

1. **Apple:** The cult of innovation

   At the core of Apple's tribe is a shared belief in innovation and sleek design. The Apple tribe identifies through a distinct language of simplicity and elegance, heroizing Steve Jobs, participating in product launch ceremonies, and displaying symbols like the iconic bitten apple.

2. **Harley-Davidson:** The open road brotherhood

   Harley-Davidson fosters a tribe built around the open road's freedom and powerful engines' roar. The Harley tribe shares a unique language of motorcycle culture symbols like the winged skull and participates in events like the Sturgis Motorcycle Rally, creating a close-knit community.

3. **Nike:** The tribe of athletic achievement

   Nike has cultivated a tribe around the pursuit of athletic excellence. With symbols like the iconic swoosh logo,

---

4 https://www.kellogg.northwestern.edu/faculty/directory/dewar_robert.aspx

heroes like Michael Jordan, and a language of victory and empowerment, the Nike tribe rallies around the brand during major sports events, turning every game into a ceremonial celebration.

4. **Tesla:** The future-focused clan

   Tesla's tribe revolves around a shared vision of a sustainable and technologically advanced future, with language emphasizing environmental consciousness, symbols like the Tesla logo, and ceremonies like Elon Musk's product unveilings—the tribe rallies behind the brand's mission.

5. **Starbucks:** The coffee connoisseur collective

   Starbucks has succeeded in creating a family of coffee lovers who derive more satisfaction from being part of the clan than just drinking coffee. The Starbucks tribe embraces a unique language of size and symbols (like the green mermaid) and participates in the ritual of ordering personalized drinks, creating a global community around a cup of coffee.

If we open this phenomenon by age and lifestyle groups, we can find examples of "tribal brands." We can Include language, symbols, and ceremonies as subtopics as important aspects because they represent powerful signs of culture that deeply influence consumer behavior and brand perception:

Language: When referring to a language spoken by a certain community or consumer segment, it goes beyond the spoken or written language, it includes both the verbal terminologies, narratives, innuendoes, or expressions frequently used by people in that community, as well as their nonverbal cues such as body language, signs, symbols, and facial expressions. Marketers will be able to effectively communicate with those in that community by paying attention to their specific languages.

Symbols: As a significant nonverbal communication tool, people are usually attracted to symbols that represent their cultures, beliefs, and ideologies. Symbols are visual representations that can convey more sensible meanings than words and verbal expressions. Companies can create logos, images, icons, etc. that vividly convey some strong messages that will resonate with their customers. For example, McDonald's icon, known as the Golden Arches, is a symbol of great dining, good customer service, and affordability. Moreover, its red color speaks of joy, family, and enjoyment.

Ceremonies: These are events or rituals that unite people from the same community for a particular purpose. When consumers participate in a ceremony linked to a brand, it can invoke in them a feeling of belongingness and cause them to be emotionally attached to the brand. Pragmatic marketers understand that promoting popular ceremonies or events can help them solidify their brand loyalty with consumers who celebrate them. When dealing with customers from different backgrounds, cultures, and communities, marketers can utilize the insights obtained from their understanding of diverse languages, symbols, and ceremonies to create marketing resources that can spark interest in their targeted market segments and cause them to be emotionally connected with the brands (and, of course, their products/services) being promoted. The following examples shed more light on this concept:

Disney: The magical kingdom

- Language: Characters, fairy tales, and magical adventures
- Symbols: Iconic characters like Mickey Mouse and the Disney Castle
- Ceremonies: Visits to Disney theme parks and princess-themed events

Dove: The self-love sisterhood

- Language: Body positivity, self-love, natural beauty
- Symbols: Dove's iconic bird logo

- Ceremonies: Dove's Real Beauty campaigns, self-care rituals

Now, let us imagine that this is a global phenomenon. These are examples by countries:

Japan:
  Toyota: The driving harmony
- Language: Precision engineering, reliability, and craftsmanship
- Symbols: Iconic Toyota logo
- Ceremonies: Annual Tokyo Motor Show, test-driving events

Adidas: The sportswear nation
- Language: Sports culture, innovation
- Symbols: Adidas' three stripes
- Ceremonies: Major sports events sponsorship, limited-edition releases

Mexico:
  Corona: The beachside fiesta
- Language: Relaxation, beach culture
- Symbols: Corona's beach sunset imagery
- Ceremonies: Summer beach parties, Corona-sponsored events

Brazil:
  Havaianas: The carnival for your feet
- Language: Vibrant colors, beach lifestyle
- Symbols: Havaianas' flip-flop designs
- Ceremonies: Carnival-themed launches, beach festivals

These brands have become cultural icons within their respective countries, connecting with consumers deeper by aligning with cultural values, traditions, and lifestyle preferences.

The tribal aspect of these brands enhances their resonance and loyalty within diverse national contexts.

5.2 Michael Porter and Consumer Behavior as a Base for Global Success

Michael Porter's idea of *"The Competitive Advantage of Nations,"* explains that a nation can become highly competitive and economically vibrant if the group or cluster of industries or companies in it are performing well. Professor Michael Porter, a well-known professor of economics at Harvard University, aimed to demonstrate that for any organization to be economically vibrant, it must be competitive against the elements of Porter's Five Forces (invented by Professor Michael Porter). The five elements of Porter's Five Framework are competitive rivalry, supplier power, buyer power, threat of substitution, and threat of new entry.

In an innovative model, I will try to merge Porter's and Dewar's ideas. My hypothesis is that tribes are the ones that create competitive industries, which in turn create successful industries within countries. Dewar's ideas should be the source of Porter's. So, "tribal" followers would in turn foster global success. Let's examine how tribal brands from the previous examples align with Porter's concept:

1. **Japan:** The video game industry cluster

    Japan has one of the most dynamic video fan tribes in the world. Nintendo has to wow this tribe and in doing so, they can wow many discerning customers around the world. Along with Nintendo, Japan has Sony, the maker of the wildly successful PlayStation line. Capcom, from Osaka, makers of Resident Evil, among others. Square Enix, makers of Final Fantasy. And we could give you many more examples. These firms have interests in the movie industry, as you can imagine, toys, merchandise, etc.

2. **Germany:**

   Germans are buyers of high-quality products based on their centuries-old engineering prowesses. The German "great engineering" tribe has helped brands like Mercedes Benz and BMW wow their local buyers, so they can easily wow international buyers as well.

3. **Mexico:** The avocado industry cluster

   These fruits are omnipresent in high-quality, exquisite Mexican cuisine. Satisfying this tribe of high-quality eaters is no simple feat. The avocado industry is a powerhouse for the Western world and creates a high-value export for this country. We could add other Mexican cuisine cases to a list, like Mexican coffee, chocolate, many salsas, tortillas, restaurants (some are US-based), etc.

These examples showcase the diversity of industry clusters within each country, with tribal brands playing a crucial role in establishing a global presence and contributing to the competitive advantage of their respective nations.

These brands successfully build tribes around shared experiences, values, and aspirations, creating a sense of community and identity within specific demographic groups. The power of tribal branding continues to shape consumer behavior, fostering deep connections and brand loyalty.

The tribal connection between these brands and their followers is nurtured through strategic branding, community-building initiatives, and shared values. Brands become symbols of identity, providing a sense of belonging and purpose. Social media platforms amplify these connections, turning brand enthusiasts into brand advocates who actively participate in the brand's rituals, ceremonies, and discussions.

In essence, the modern tribe effect showcases how brands, like the tribes of old, have the power to bring people together, foster a sense of identity, and create communities that transcend mere consumerism. As consumers increasingly seek belonging and shared values, the phenomenon of brand tribes continues to shape the intricate landscape of consumer behavior.

5.3 The Jones Effect

The Jones effect, deeply ingrained in the fabric of human behavior, finds its roots in social comparison. Coined from the popular expression "keeping up with the Joneses," this effect delves into our intrinsic tendency to evaluate ourselves based on others' possessions, achievements, or lifestyles. Let's unravel the layers of the Jones effect, exploring its discovery and how it shapes our consumer landscape.

The concept gained prominence in the early 20th century, attributed to the American cartoonist Arthur R. "Pop" Momand. In 1913, he introduced a cartoon strip titled "Keeping up with the Joneses," portraying the social pressure to emulate the material success of neighbors, the Jones family. While Momand's creation primarily focused on suburban rivalry, the underlying psychological dynamics evolved into a broader phenomenon.

The Jones effect draws heavily from Festinger's social comparison theory[5]. Festinger proposed that individuals determine their social and personal standing by comparing themselves to others. The drive to conform and avoid feelings of inadequacy or inferiority fuels this comparative process.

The key concepts involved in this theory are:

1. **Social identity:** This refers to individuals' traits as associated with certain "tribes", and this identity is usually reflected in common beliefs, interests, characteristics, or values shared by the members of the tribes. Brands

---

5 Leon Festiger, "Social Comparison Processes: Theoretical and Empirical Perspectives", 1954.

can usually step in to be a unifier of people in a tribe by promoting their culture and social events.

2. **Cultural narratives:** Brands construct unique narratives, symbols, and ceremonies akin to tribal traditions. Consumers further adopt these cultural elements, fostering a shared identity within the brand community.

3. **Aspirational influence:** The Jones effect thrives on aspirational motivations, prompting individuals to align their choices with those they perceive as aspirational figures. Heroes within a brand's narrative contribute to this aspirational influence.

The Jones effect significantly influences purchasing decisions, lifestyle choices, and brand affiliations. The desire to keep pace with or surpass perceived peers motivates consumers to acquire products or experiences associated with their chosen tribes. Marketers strategically leverage this effect to create aspirational brand identities and cultivate loyalty.

5.3.1 Contemporary relevance of the Jones effect

In today's hyper-connected world, the Jones effect has found new dimensions through social media, where curated images of lifestyles and possessions intensify the comparison game. Brands strategically position themselves as markers of status and identity, capitalizing on the innate human inclination to belong and measure one's worth within a social context.

Understanding the intricacies of the Jones effect equips marketers with the insights needed to craft compelling brand narratives, fostering connections beyond products – they become symbols of identity, aspiration, and tribal belonging in the ever-evolving landscape of consumer behavior.

The Jones Effect, a powerful psychological influence, motivates consumers to acquire products or services based on the desire to keep up with or impress others. Brands can leverage this effect to cultivate brand loyalty and a sense of belonging. Let's delve into two prime examples:

1. **GoPro:** Adventure Awaits (Social Proof and Aspiration)

   GoPro doesn't just sell cameras; it sells a lifestyle. Their marketing focuses on capturing and sharing extraordinary experiences. When GoPro publishes user-generated content on its website and official social media platforms, it excites readers and causes them to consider GoPro (camera) as a very useful tool for adventures and active lifestyle.

   Therefore, consumers who bought GoPro understood that they were not just purchasing a camera but actually buying into a community. They presumed that they already belonged to a tribe of pleasure-seeking adventurers and explorers who are pushing boundaries and are happy to share their documented, great experiences with others using their cameras. This social proof and aspirational association fuel the Jones Effect, driving consumers to join the GoPro community.

2. **Patagonia:** Sustainable Style (Values and Identity)

   The brand caters to a different aspect of the Jones Effect. The brand champions environmental consciousness and outdoor exploration. Their commitment to sustainability resonates with a specific audience who identify with a love for nature and ethical consumerism. Owning Patagonia apparel becomes a way to express these values and project a particular identity.

   The values mentioned above gave Patagonia the unique opportunity to impress upon its customers that they are environmentally friendly by using a product from a company that respects and identifies with such an environmental sustainability value. This social influence motivates others to purchase Patagonia products, further strengthening the brand's position and community.

In conclusion, both GoPro and Patagonia strategically leverage the Jones Effect. GoPro concentrates on users' desires to experience great adventures and join the community of like-minded adventurers, while Patagonia's customers align themselves with the company's values of environmental sustainability. These two companies with two different products are able to psychologically influence their customers' emotions and choices, and this approach is a viable marketing strategy that many companies are still utilizing today.

5.5 Social Media and The Digital Tribe

Social media platforms like Facebook, Twitter (now X), Instagram, and TikTok are playing significant roles in the creation and perpetuation of digital tribes. Nowadays, tribe members can organize virtual campfires, participate in online social events, and virtually go on adventures together. The application of Jones' effect can be seen in all these examples, and it is no longer weird for total strangers to connect with one another, share personal information, and perceive themselves as members of the same tribe. With this interesting development, social media affords companies the opportunity to study consumers' trends, behaviors, and emotional requirements so as to target them with the most appropriate marketing types that will resonate with them. Let's take a look at the following examples from the social media world:

1. **Instagram's visual tribes:**

   Instagram facilitates the creation of digital tribes by encouraging users to tell compelling, visual stories about themselves, their experiences, and day-to-day living. From influencers to social media hobbyists, their well-crafted messages are able to encourage people to form communities of like-minded people, comprising those who share the same interests, ideologies, and aesthetics. The Jones effect manifests through the aspirational nature of visually driven content as tribes compete to set and follow trends.

2. **TikTok's cultural phenomenon:**

Since TikTok came to the scene, its wide acceptance by the public reveals that many users perceive it as an alternative to Instagram, posting short videos and alluring images that depict their everyday lifestyles, hobbies, etc. People with similar characteristics tend to form communities and tribes on TikTok, exchanging or sharing curated content that helps them remain active members of their respective communities.

The platform's algorithmic approach ensures content discovery aligns with user preferences, fueling the Jones effect as tribes strive to stay in sync with the latest viral sensations.

Collectively, these digital campfires play a pivotal role in shaping consumer aspirations. The Jones effect manifests through creating trends influencing attitudes toward products, lifestyles, and cultural phenomena. The digital tribes around these platforms contribute to a nuanced understanding of modern consumer behavior, reflecting the constant desire to align with and outshine the digital "Joneses" in their respective tribes.

It is now clear that companies that understand and explore how communities are formed on social media can take advantage of this phenomenon to reach out to these communities, positively influence their behaviors through emotional motivations, and turn them into loyal patrons or customers.

5.6 Applying Tribal Concepts to Your Business

Incorporating concepts related to tribal consumers into your business strategies involves recognizing the communal nature of consumer behavior and tailoring your approach accordingly. Here are additional steps:

1. **Community-centric marketing:** It is advisable that brands should position themselves mostly as community facilitator online, rather than promoters and sellers of products/ services for people to buy. It is equally important to foster a sense of belongingness among the community members by highlighting common values, beliefs, and interests.

2. **Create exclusive communities:** Establish exclusive online communities or forums dedicated to your brand. These spaces provide tribal consumers a platform to connect, share experiences, and engage with your brand on a deeper level.

3. **Customize products for tribes:** Consider creating special editions or customizing products based on the preferences of specific tribes. This approach not only meets the unique needs of tribal consumers but also strengthens their identification with your brand.

4. **Celebrate tribe milestones:** Acknowledge and celebrate milestones within your tribal consumer community. One of the most effective approaches for fostering a sense of pride and loyalty among consumers is for brands to periodically, when necessary, celebrate their own achievements as well as recognize and promote events and ceremonies that the community members are quite passionate about.

5. **Interactive tribal content:** Develop content that encourages interaction among tribal consumers. To encourage active engagement on social media platforms, brands can utilize quizzes, competitions, polls, etc. This will make consumers feel valued and wholly involved in the community-building efforts.

6. **Highlight tribe influencers:** Showcase influencers from within your tribal community. Using influencers who are already part of the tribe and share in the common vision can help organizations create realistic content and invoke a feeling of authenticity and trustworthiness in other tribe members.

7. **Organize tribal events:** Host virtual or physical events that bring tribal consumers together. This could include product launches, live Q&A sessions, or themed gatherings reinforcing the sense of community.

8. **Feedback loop with tribes:** Establish a continuous feedback loop with your tribal consumers. Actively seek their opinions on product development, marketing campaigns, and overall brand experience. This not only values their input but also strengthens the bond.

9. **Tribal loyalty programs:** Tribe members can be motivated to proactively engage with a brand's social media platforms and even make regular purchases if there are loyalty programs, perks, and early access models designed to reward active community members, who routinely participate in discussions, leave comments, and post some images.

10. **Empower tribal leaders:** Identify and empower tribal leaders within your consumer community. These individuals naturally influence others and can play a pivotal role in shaping the narrative around your brand.

11. **Storytelling with tribal narratives:** Incorporate tribal narratives into your brand storytelling. Share stories of how your products/services positively impact the lives of tribal consumers, creating a shared narrative that strengthens the tribal bond.

12. **Cross-tribal collaborations:** Explore collaborations with other brands that resonate with your tribal consumers. It is generally believed that promoting cross-tribal engagements

can expand an organization's reach to a previously untapped customer base.

It is possible for businesses to win the hearts of consumers and subsequently retain them if they focus on fostering engagement within inter-tribal communities and supporting events that are related to the community members. People are often emotionally attached to things that they care about, and this provides an effective marketing opportunity for businesses. This approach goes beyond transactions, building enduring relationships within the interconnected landscape of digital tribes.

Quiz

━━

1. **Consumer behavior extends the concept of tribes beyond traditional anthropology by emphasizing**

    a. Individual purchasing decisions

    b. Social media engagement

    c. Shared cultural identities

    d. Market research insights

2. **Professor Robert Dewar's research highlights modern tribes in**

    a. Political affiliations

    b. Brand loyalty

    c. Academic circles

    d. Online gaming communities

3. **Brands like Apple, Harley-Davidson, Nike, Tesla, and Starbucks evoke cult-like followings akin to**

    a. Corporate mergers

    b. Religious organizations

    c. Scientific research groups

    d. Political parties

4. **Shared language, symbols, heroes, ceremonies, and identifications create a sense of belonging among**

    a. Brand managers

    b. Advertising agencies

    c. Tribal communities

    d. Government agencies

5. **Examples across demographics and regions illustrate how brands become**
   a. Cultural artifacts
   b. Investment opportunities
   c. Legal entities
   d. Social networks

6. **Tribes play a crucial role in shaping consumer behavior by fostering**
   a. Indifference
   b. Deep connections and loyalty
   c. Short-term trends
   d. Product recalls

7. **What is a key characteristic of brands that evoke cult-like followings?**
   a. Low-quality products
   b. High pricing
   c. Strong emotional connections
   d. Limited availability

8. **How do shared languages, symbols, and ceremonies contribute to brand loyalty?**
   a. They encourage individualism
   b. They foster a sense of belonging
   c. They promote competition
   d. They discourage consumer engagement

9. **The concept of "Brand Loyalty as Tribal Affiliation" refers to**

    a. Consumers feel obligated to buy a brand's products

    b. Consumers develop a strong sense of belonging with a brand

    c. Brands offer discounts to loyal customers

    d. Brands target specific demographics for loyalty programs

10. **Which of the following brands is NOT mentioned in the passage as an example of a brand with a passionate following resembling a tribe?**

    a. Apple

    b. Microsoft

    c. Nike

    d. Tesla

Answers	1 – d	2 – d	3 – b	4 – c	5 – a
	6 – b	7 – c	8 – b	9 – b	10 – b

Chapter Summary

◆ Consumer tribes extend the traditional anthropological concept to encompass brand loyalty.

◆ Research by Robert Dewar identifies the rise of modern tribes formed around shared brand passion.

◆ Brands like Apple, Harley-Davidson, Nike, Tesla, and Starbucks cultivate devoted followings similar to ancient tribes.

◆ Elements fostering tribal affiliation include shared language (slogans), symbols (logos), heroes (founders), rituals (product launches), and a strong sense of brand identity.

◆ Brand tribes influence consumer behavior by building deep connections and loyalty that transcends the product itself.

Further Reading

Refer to the following videos to enhance understanding of the concepts and examples discussed in this chapter. Links to these videos are also available in the Online Resources section of this book.

- Lululemon's marketing strategy: https://www.youtube.com/watch?v=_FeJQc5ws8Y

- Lululemon's success as a business: https://www.youtube.com/watch?v=tItUlA1C_So

- Havaianas, Brazil's success story: https://www.youtube.com/watch?v=wniD75E1vIg

- Avocados from Mexico marketing strategy: https://www.youtube.com/watch?v=umW-N-RmRxI

- Harley Davidson's marketing strategy: https://www.youtube.com/watch?v=9lvlKBJ1Tss

Case Study: Tesla Vs Byd: Analysis Of Their "Tribes" And Strategies

The Electric Revolution: A Charged Landscape for Tesla and BYD

The roar of gasoline engines is slowly giving way to the quiet hum of electric motors. The electric vehicle (EV) market is experiencing explosive growth, driven by a confluence of factors:

- Environmental concerns: Climate change is a pressing issue, and consumers are increasingly seeking sustainable transportation options. EVs offer a significant reduction in tailpipe emissions.
- Technological advancements: Battery technology is improving rapidly, offering EVs with longer ranges and shorter charging times.
- Government incentives: Many governments are offering subsidies and tax breaks to promote EV adoption, making them more affordable for consumers.
- Shifting consumer preferences: Consumers are becoming more aware of the environmental impact of their choices and are drawn to the sleek design and futuristic appeal of EVs.

However, the new EV market isn't without its realities, which are as follows:

- Cost parity: While production costs are coming down, EVs generally have a higher upfront cost compared to gasoline-powered vehicles.
- Charging infrastructure: The availability of charging stations, particularly fast-charging options, is still limited in many areas, causing range anxiety for potential EV buyers.

- Supply chain challenges: The global chip shortage and the reliance on specific raw materials for batteries can hinder EV production.
- Competition heats up: Traditional automakers are joining the fray, offering a wider range of EV models at various price points. This intensifies competition for Tesla and BYD, the current leaders in the EV space.

This case study dives into the strategies of Tesla and BYD, the two titans battling for dominance in this dynamic and rapidly evolving electric vehicle market. We'll analyze their strengths and weaknesses, their target markets, and their approaches to navigating the realities of this exciting new frontier in transportation.

The road ahead

Tesla and BYD are constantly innovating and expanding. Tesla continues to develop self-driving technology, introduce new models like the Cybertruck and Model Y, and explore robotics with Tesla Optimus. BYD, meanwhile, is aiming to increase its global presence and compete head-on with Tesla in the premium EV segment.

The electric vehicle (EV) market is diverse, and both Tesla and BYD cater to distinct customer segments. Let's explore their target markets through the lens of demographics, attitudes, behaviors, and aspirations:

Tesla: Targeting the eco-conscious tech-savvy

Demographics: Affluent professionals, early adopters of technology, aged 35-55 with higher education levels and disposable income.

Attitudes: Environmentally conscious, value sustainability and innovation. They believe electric vehicles are a symbol of progress and responsible consumption.

Behaviors: Actively research new technologies, and appreciate cutting-edge features like autonomous driving and long-range.

They are comfortable with online research and direct-to-consumer sales models.

Aspirational: Owning a Tesla signifies a connection to a forward-thinking, sustainable lifestyle. It reflects a desire to be at the forefront of technological advancement and contribute to a cleaner future.

BYD: Balancing Affordability and Practicality

Demographics: A broader range than Tesla, including environmentally conscious consumers and budget-minded individuals seeking practical transportation solutions. Age groups may skew slightly younger due to affordability considerations.

Attitudes: Value for money is important. They appreciate the environmental benefits of EVs but prioritize practicality and affordability.

Behaviors: Conduct research online and offline, influenced by dealership recommendations. They may be open to alternative fuel vehicles but find EVs increasingly appealing.

Aspirational: Owning a BYD signifies a responsible choice – environmentally friendly transportation without breaking the bank. It represents a practical and sustainable way to participate in the electric vehicle revolution.

Here's a table summarizing the key differences:

Feature	Tesla	BYD
Demographics	Affluent, tech-savvy	Broader range, budget-minded
Attitudinal	Eco-conscious, innovative	Value, practical, environment
Behavioral	Online research, direct-to-consumer	Online & offline research, dealerships
Aspirational	Cutting-edge, sustainable	Practical, affordable, sustainable

Case Study Questions for Tesla vs. BYD

This case study delves into the strategies of Tesla and BYD, the frontrunners in the electric vehicle revolution. To gain a deeper understanding of their approaches and target markets, consider these thought-provoking questions:

1. **Strategic advantage:** While both Tesla and BYD prioritize innovation, their approaches differ. Analyze which company's strategy – Tesla's focus on premium, high-tech EVs or BYD's emphasis on affordability and market diversification – seems more sustainable in the long term. Why?

2. **Target market evolution:** As the EV market matures and charging infrastructure expands, how do you see the target markets for Tesla and BYD evolving? Will the demographic and behavioral profiles of their ideal customers shift?

3. **Emerging technologies:** Both companies are heavily invested in research and development. How might the integration of new technologies like solid-state batteries or alternative charging solutions impact Tesla and BYD's competitiveness?

4. **Global expansion:** While Tesla has a presence in many countries, BYD's focus has been more on China. How can BYD leverage its strengths to effectively compete with Tesla in international markets?

5. **Imagine the tribe:** Close your eyes and envision the ideal customer for each company. Describe their:

    *   **Language:** What kind of words and phrases would they use to talk about electric vehicles?
    *   **Symbols:** What images or logos would resonate with them?
    *   **Influencers:** Who are the celebrities or social media personalities they look up to?

- **Events:** What kind of conferences, trade shows, or experiences would they be drawn to?

By pondering these questions and delving into the case study, you'll gain a comprehensive understanding of Tesla and BYD's strategies, their target markets, and their potential paths to success in the ever-evolving electric vehicle landscape.

This page is intentionally left blank

Chapter **6**

Marketing Research and Customer Behavior

C hapter six shows that in the intricate landscape of consumer behavior, the beacon guiding businesses is illuminated by the fusion of marketing research and the understanding of customer behavior. This chapter delves into why this symbiotic relationship is not merely essential but a strategic imperative for any business aiming for sustainable success.

Key learning objectives should include the reader's understanding of the following:

- Defining marketing research and decoding the customer's mind
- The power of insights
- The art and science of surveys
- Interpreting responses

6.1 Marketing Research: The Informed Navigator

Marketing research is described as the process of gathering, analyzing, and interpreting consumers' information or data for the singular purpose of understanding their behaviors and market dynamics. Businesses utilize marketing research to navigate new and existing marketplaces and explore opportunities for growth. This chapter explains how businesses can achieve their goals by proactively adopting well-coordinated marketing research.

Imagine you are a driver going to a crucial meeting without a map or GPS. You may ask for directions along the way, but you may need clarification on guidelines from the non-experienced. You may get perfectly clear directions, but that will generally depend on sheer luck. The most thoughtful process would be to gather as much information about the road to take, think about all the contingencies that may come up and prepare for those (maybe check your car state, the spare tire is inflated, among others), and leave all ready and prepared in the morning. This is a perfect analogy for working with marketing research or going your way to pure luck. Imagine who gets there first!

A critical element to this story is something that I always tell my students and clients. Marketing research typically can be managed with very reasonable budgets. You need not be a large corporation to have decent market information. What is always important is that research passes the test of reasonability and creativity. What do I mean by that? That you understand that information is reasonable, including possible downsides to it. And creativity means finding new ways to measure market phenomena within time and budget constraints.

Even though different businesses utilize marketing research in different ways, they seem to be targeting the same goals — having the ability to extract useful information about consumers, such as their preferences, buying patterns, and the nature of decision-making. Businesses, in turn, will use these data to make informed decisions that will put them ahead of their rivals having learned about their customers' wants and purchasing trends. The informed navigator helps managers steer toward success in a competitive landscape.

We will explain real-world examples where businesses, armed with insights from marketing research, made strategic decisions that propelled them ahead of competitors. From product innovations to market expansions, upcoming case studies highlight the tangible impact of effective marketing research in navigating the complex terrain of consumer behavior.

In essence, this chapter will serve as a guideline, introducing businesses to the compass of marketing research. It beckons them to embark on a journey of discovery, where understanding consumer behavior becomes the key to charting a course toward sustainable success.

6.2 Decoding the Customer's Mind

There are real-world examples to ascertain that businesses that undertake marketing research are usually equipped with the right amount of business insights that they can employ in refining their business practices, increasing efficiency, and expanding their customer base accordingly.

With the following examples, we unravel compelling tales of strategic metamorphosis ignited by a deep understanding of customer behavior.

6.2.1 Zara: Fast fashion tailored to consumer desires

Zara's success as a fast-fashion empire is attributable to the marketing research it routinely undertakes. The practical insights obtained from this research help Zara respond proactively to changes in consumers' needs, preferences, and fashion trends. The company utilizes the information/data from its marketing research to acknowledge the ever-evolving transformations in the fashion industry and produce clothes that are current and meet consumers' needs.

The following factors explain why Zara remains a leader in the fast-fashion industry:

- **Fast-fashion and trend responsiveness:** One main factor that has made Zara a sustainable business model is that it quickly responds to its customers' ever-changing fashion preferences and trends. Not only that, but it also makes fast fashion accessible and affordable to those who need it.

- **Limited production and scarcity:** The concept of product scarcity has been employed by Zara to make its clothing items appear exclusive, luxurious, and unique. Consumers like purchasing quickly products that are scarce because it gives them the impression, psychologically, that they are unique products that are only made available to special customers.

- **Data-driven decision-making:** Utilizing information obtained from ongoing marketing research, data analytics, and insights from consumers' behaviors and feedback, Zara has been paying attention to its customers' changing needs and trends, supplying them with the exact fashion styles that they require, and keeping up with their other fashion demands.

- **In-store experience and merchandising:** Zara's attractive in-store design and visually appealing merchandising encourage consumers to immediately make purchasing decisions when inside any of Zara's stores. They buy their desired clothes very quickly realizing that Zara has a regularly changing inventory, and some clothing items on display this week may disappear a few weeks later owing to Zara's strategic placement of its clothing items. Zara may have intentionally or unintentionally encouraged this impulse buying, but it is very clear that the company responds quickly to changes in its customers' preferences and needs.

6.2.2 BMW: Driving luxury with consumer insights

Well known for its comfortable and flashy automobiles, BMW remains a leader in the luxury automobile industry simply because it harnesses the power and insights of marketing research to deliver a streamlined and aesthetic line of luxury cars that its customers are happy to associate with and want. Buying a BMW car is mostly perceived among BMW users as a lifestyle choice.

- **Brand image and aspirational appeal:** The BMW brand is popular for delivering cars that embody luxury, innovation, and performance, giving its customers the prestige of driving pleasurably around in state-of-the-art automobiles.
- **Product customization and personalization:** BMW stays ahead of other manufacturers of luxury automobiles by offering a service that allows current and prospective customers to customize their dream cars as they desire, as permitted by the company's technology. This high-level customization or personalization of cars gives BMW users a feeling of being individually in charge of meeting their automobile preferences or needs.
- **Innovative technology and performance:** To actualize its customers' important preferences for a comfortable driving experience coupled with their love for advanced vehicular technologies, BMW incorporates the latest automobile features and technologies in its cars in order to achieve high vehicular performance.
- **Effective marketing and communication:** One of BMW's popular marketing slogans, the "Ultimate Driving Machine" evokes a combined feeling of luxury and performance in consumers. BMW customers are constantly reminded, through marketing communications, that they are not only purchasing a means of transportation but also subscribing to a lifestyle of comfort and superb driving experience.

- **Sustainability initiatives:** BMW is at the forefront of automobile manufacturers embracing sustainability in all their practices. With the production of its BMW i Series, the company has ventured into the manufacturing of electric and hybrid cars that are environmentally friendly, energy-efficient, and safe.

Despite being a very competitive industry, BMW has been able to maintain its leadership in the automobile market because of its apparent incorporation of innovation and marketing research in its operations, providing sustainable products to its luxury-seeking customers and enhancing their comfort, safety, and driving experiences.

6.2.3 Salesforce.com: Revolutionizing CRM with data-driven precision

Salesforce, a customer relationship management (CRM) company, helps businesses to have unrestricted access to their customers' data so that they can track their interactions and have a 30-degree view of the sales data arising from the customers' transactions. Salesforce literally simplifies the processes of finding new leads, contacts, and opportunities. Moreover, businesses can entirely automate these procedures for faster and more efficient execution.

Some of the factors that have largely contributed to Salesforce's success are highlighted below:

- **Cloud-based solutions:** Salesforce can be considered a pioneer of cloud-based CRM solutions. The company has been able to provide scalable, affordable, and flexible cloud-based customer relationship management solutions that most businesses require as they migrate from inflexible, traditional on-premises CRM software to agile and customizable approaches.
- **Customer-centric approach:** Salesforce has always worked toward ensuring that its clients attain a high rate of success and satisfaction in their CRM efforts. The

company achieves this goal by making its platform to be user-friendly with CRM features and capabilities that are customizable.

- **Innovation and acquisitions:** By acquiring Slack (a streamlined business communications tool) and Tableau (a powerful data visualization software), Salesforce is actively investing in innovation and making strategic moves to remain a leading CRM solution provider in the ever-dynamic customer relationship management (CRM) industry.
- **Community engagement:** The Salesforce software is primarily designed to foster a strong community among users, administrators, developers, and partners collaborating on a project together. With features like Trailhead and Dreamforce, the company creates a thriving ecosystem where it engages with its clientele, users of its software, and those learning about the Salesforce comprehensive concept for CRM.
- **Adaptation to remote work trends:** Salesforce makes collaboration between on-site and offsite (virtual) workers easier with its features that support the shift to modern, remote working environments.

Salesforce's adoption has steadily increased over the years as both the existing and new users appreciate and take advantage of the company's offerings and capabilities, such as its cloud-based model, creation of engaged communities, investment in innovation and acquisitions, adaptability to remote working lifestyles, and its customer-centric approaches.

6.2.4 Samsung: Innovating consumer electronics with insights

As a multinational electronics company, Samsung has managed to stay on top of the industry by utilizing marketing research to refine and modify its line of products including televisions, smartphones, consumer products, and home appliances. There is no doubt that Samsung acts on the insights from its routine research and development (R&D) to make products that consumers desire, which are functional, durable, aesthetic, and cost-effective.

- **Galaxy S Series:** To differentiate its smartphones from others like Apple's iPhones and Xiaomi's Redmi, Samsung Galaxy S Series phones contain all the preferred features and functionalities by high-taste smartphone users, such as beautiful, sleek design, high-resolution cameras, sophisticated processors, and enhanced displays. Its new S24 Series (scheduled for launching) comes with AI functionality and better performance.

- **Curved edge display:** The curved edge display enhances Samsung smartphones' usability and aesthetics. This feature provides a shortcut for users to quickly access any applications on their smartphones. In addition to that, it makes it possible for users to immediately see notifications and updates on their phones. The curved edge display undoubtedly enables users to smoothly interact with their devices and make good use of them.

- **Samsung Galaxy buds:** When Samsung joined the race to produce wireless audio earbuds, it primarily focused on making wireless buds that will meet consumers' expectations by providing absolute convenience and usability/functionality. Since the introduction of its Galaxy Buds Series to the market, Samsung has continued to revolutionize this product, winning the hearts of delicate consumers seeking continuous convenience.

- **QLED TVs and Lifestyle TVs:** What separates Samsung's QLED TVs from the others in the market are that they possess great display technology, better contrast ratios, and admirable color and picture quality. Similarly, Samsung's lifestyle TVs, The Frame, and The

Serif add beauty to consumers' living spaces as they are aesthetically designed to challenge rivals' existing home electronics.

- **Innovation in home appliances:** Samsung has manufactured some innovative home appliances aimed at bringing convenience to consumers and increasing their efficiency at home. Groundbreaking products such as Family Hub refrigerators come with built-in touchscreens, and FlexWash washing machines and smart ovens revealed Samsung's technical advancement in meeting consumers' needs with products that can alleviate some of their home-based concerns.

Samsung has secured its esteemed place in the global electronics market owing to its strict adherence to standards, aesthetics, marketing research, and supplying consumers' needs based on their preferences for high-tech and high-performance home appliances, smartphones, and electronics products.

6.2.5 YouTube: Personalized content discovery

Against all odds, YouTube has consistently utilized insights from its marketing research to provide users with engaging content or videos they are mostly interested in watching. The company was able to achieve this feat through data-driven algorithms that feed users with the appropriate videos/content based on their specific behaviors, historical preferences, and viewing habits. These individualized, user-centric recommendations keep people glued to YouTube for several hours a day.

- **Diverse content ecosystem:** YouTube successfully keeps users engaged by providing content/videos that meet their diverse requirements or needs, covering different genres like education, lifestyle, music, entertainment, and others. Since there is usually something for everyone to enjoy on the platform,

YouTube continues to be one of the most popular social media in the world.

- **YouTube creators and influencers:** By offering its platform as a springboard for many creators and influencers, YouTube has consistently attracted all kinds of audiences that desire to have relevant, educational, and entertaining content/videos. The caliber of creators and influencers on YouTube ranges from amateur to professional musicians, gamers, vloggers, educationists, personal finance advisors, etc., all regularly making content/videos users are searching for.

- **Monetization opportunities:** Allowing creators and influencers to monetize their content has been a game-changing move by YouTube. The most important aspect of the company's Partner Program and monetization opportunities is that YouTube makes it readily easy for people to financially support their favorite creators and influencers through ads, merchandise shelf options, and membership subscriptions.

- **Live streaming and interaction:** By supporting live streaming and consummate interactions between creators and their audiences, YouTube has further expanded its community-building initiatives. Livestreams offer creators and influencers a unique opportunity to engage in real-time with their audiences, deepening their existing interactions. This aligns with the growing desire for interactive and participatory content consumption.

- **YouTube premium:** With its Premium subscription service, YouTube also caters to the needs of users who don't want to be hampered or disturbed by disruptive ads while enjoying their favorite content/videos on the platform. The Premium subscription offers ad-free, offline viewing, and unrestricted access to YouTube Originals.

- **Global accessibility:** YouTube's availability across devices, languages, and regions contributes to its international success. The platform recognizes the importance of accessibility, allowing users worldwide to consume content in their preferred languages and genres. Connecting people from their cultures and walks of life helps categorize YouTube as one of the most inclusive social media across the world.

Over the years, despite the emerging competition from other video-hosting or live-streaming platforms, YouTube continues to be successful or do well on every metric due to its superb services that seamlessly connect people from different corners of the world. As a digital ecosystem, users find pleasure in consuming useful and entertaining digital content/videos on the platform, and its innovative features that facilitate easy upload of content and monetization keep creators, influencers, and their audiences ever busy on the platform.

6.2.6 Nestlé: Crafting culinary experiences with consumer understanding

Nestle has survived the intense competition in the food industry to become a global leader owing to its persistent marketing research and data-driven decision-making. Taking into consideration cultural nuances and ever-changing dietary trends, Nestle offers a combination of food products that appeal to consumers' tastes and recognize individual cultural sensitivities. This approach, without doubt, helps the company to stretch across different geographical locations and cultures.

- **Nespresso:** Nespresso is Nestle's premium coffee brand, and it offers consumers who like premium coffee some convenience and enjoyable coffee experience. With the introduction of premium coffee capsules and machines, Nestle captivates a consumer segment that prides itself on quality and enjoyable coffee.
- **Kit Kat:** Nestle used its memorable *"Have a Break, Have a Kit Kat "* campaign to enlighten consumers that the

company cares about their well-being and that having enough relaxation can refresh their body systems. By tapping into consumers' emotional requirements or preferences, Nestle positions itself as a company that understands what consumers really want. This feeling of being cared for might explain why Kit Kat is a very popular brand.

- **Nestle's Pure Life:** Nestle's purified water brand is a strategic response to consumers' desire to drink healthy beverages. Over the years, there has been an increasing demand for purified water, and Pure Life is Nestle's solution to this issue.

- **Maggi:** From its instant soups, noodles, and seasonings, Nestle's Maggi is well known all over the world, and these products have been adapted to suit consumers' diverse tastes across many cultures. Consumers who desire to enjoy convenient and fast cooking often prefer Nestle's meal solutions.

- **Health Science Division:** Nestle understands, from its marketing research and data analysis, that there has been an uptick in the number of health-conscious consumers. By providing nutritional supplements and healthy food products, Nestle positions itself as a company that knows exactly what consumers desire, doing everything it takes to take good care of them health-wise.

By making innovative products that consumers admire, Nestle continues to grow successfully while maintaining a positive brand image. Moreover, consumers appreciate its useful products or solutions that meet their individual needs/preferences.

Each of the examples above demonstrates how businesses can utilize marketing research and insights about consumer behaviors to plan their operations, innovate their products/services, and maintain a leading position in their respective industries.

6.3 The Art and Science of Surveys

In this digital age, survey creation has changed from the previous, paper-based survey design to the fast, internet-based one. With survey applications such as SurveyMonkey, Google Forms, Qualtrics, and Typeform, survey creators can quickly craft surveys they can use to obtain vital data that will be analyzed, interpreted, and used for significant decision-making.

6.3.1 Old vs. new survey creation methods

This section critically looks at the old and new ways of designing surveys and highlights their different approaches.

Old methods: The traditional method of surveying requires the use of paper questionnaires on which respondents are required to tick their opinions or responses. This method seems error-prone and cumbersome because it takes a lot of time to administer the surveys, gather data from them, and subsequently analyze them. The only merit of this practice is that it allows face-to-face consultations and it could add more human feeling/emotion to the surveying process.

New methods: On the other hand, internet-based or online surveys like Google Forms and SurveyMonkey are fast, convenient, and mostly error-free. It affords the organizer of the survey a unique opportunity to collect data from a large population of respondents, irrespective of their locations. Moreover, the data collection, analysis, and interpretation processes are streamlined and efficient.

No modern marketer can stand outside this new era where internet/social media surveys can be performed quickly and cheaply. There are alternative methods that complement what an online survey can bring. But let us discuss the pros and cons of these methods.

Table 6.1	**Pros and cons of online survey apps**

	Pros	Cons
SurveyMonkey	1. User-friendly interface 2. Advanced features 3. Extensive template library for different purposes	1. Limited free version 2. Relatively expensive pricing
Google Forms	1. Free 2. Seamlessly integrates with Google Workspace 3. Enables easy collaboration with real-time editing	1. Only basic features 2. Limited design options

Table 6.1 shows the pros and cons of SurveyMonkey and Google Forms, two popularly used survey tools. SurveyMonkey possesses an intuitive design that makes it easy for users to smoothly create their surveys. Additionally, it has some advanced features that facilitate the art of designing surveys. A particular example of these features is advanced branching logic—this allows survey creators to use respondents' past answers to create an entirely new survey. Hence, respondents will only be served survey questions that are closely related to the previous responses. It is also possible to export data from the app and integrate it with other software such as CRM systems and analytical tools for optimized functionality.

On the other hand, Google Forms is entirely free to use and provides good integration and collaboration options. However, it lacks some advanced features present in other platforms and has limited design options.

As we bid farewell to traditional survey methods embracing the efficiency of online applications, weighing each platform's pros and cons is essential. Whether using SurveyMonkey, Google Forms, or other tools, understanding the nuances of data interpretation ensures the extraction of valuable insights, steering businesses toward informed decision-making in the digital age.

6.3.2 Interpreting survey data

Interpreting survey data is a crucial aspect of deriving meaningful insights. Tools such as Google Forms provide a basic analysis of the survey inputs. However, more sophisticated statistical tools can also be used to generate meaningful insights. Some key considerations include:

1. **Segmentation:** Analyze the data based on demographics or respondent characteristics for targeted insights.
2. **Comparisons:** Compare responses across different survey questions to identify patterns.
3. **Statistical analysis:** Utilize statistical tools to derive correlations and trends.
4. **Visualization:** Visualize data through charts and graphs for more precise interpretation.
5. **Feedback analysis:** Pay attention to open-ended responses for qualitative insights.

6.4 Market Research: Applications For Your Business

Defining which marketing research method is best for your business requires technical knowledge, cost analysis, and a bit of art too! The best tool, if poorly applied, is never the best option.

My recommendation is "think about your problem first". When you start at that point, you will be better positioned to think about the tool and how to apply it. Here is a list of some common problems businesses might face and some recommendations.

1. **New product/new packaging introduction:**
   - It can be advisable to show prototypes or samples for them to see, taste or use, depending on the product or service.

- Consumers will rarely be able to give you much information about a product they have not yet used because they are not experts.
- Consider a test market for your new product and learn from it.
- All tests at this level are qualitative, not quantitative. This means that results are difficult to project the total population.
- Beware of "socially correct answers". Consumers tend to reply that what you are showing them is good because they do not want to be rude to the interviewer. Present alternatives, like two flavors, one is the one you want to test, for them to rank. Little trick among many.

2. **Price changes in your product:**

- To test what price would best fit your product, I would suggest presenting interviewees with alternatives, almost always. What I say here is, to have people choose between pairs of options like, Hotel A at $200/night vs Hotel B at $300/ night with a list of features for each. They are not choosing prices alone (assuming you want to test that here) but a complete set of features, more like what happens in real life.
- There are more sophisticated tools with this perspective, but within the perspective of this book, I am happy to remind people that choices are normally made with multiple options in place.

3. **Customers pain points:**

- This is a great way to improve products or services and define improvements.
- You can use statistical information on warranty claims, if applicable. Otherwise, it is great to contact recent users to check on what they find should be improved in your service.
- Mystery shoppers are a great way to check your business quality.

- Talk to your front-line employees frequently and have them rank issues for you.

4. **Competitive analysis:**

- Focus groups are a wonderful way to understand how consumers look at your brand vs competitors. This interaction is great to understand how they speak about your product.

- An online focus group is more difficult to achieve because I question how "focused" the participants are. Yet, you can review social media with your experts and get gold-quality information.

5. **Advertising effectiveness in social media:**

- Statistical and qualitative analysis are fundamental in determining how efficient your strategy has been in producing sales, likes, or followers, whatever your original goal was.

Refer to the Online Resources section of the book to access practical hands-on exercises related to the concepts in the chapter and a list of additional tools to study consumer behavior.

Quiz

1. **The reason why marketing research is often compared to a compass is that it can help businesses**

   a. Develop creative marketing campaigns

   b. Navigate the complexities of the business landscape

   c. Manage production costs efficiently

   d. Boost employees' morale

2. **How does marketing research impact strategic decision-making?**

   a. It cuts down the number of employees required in the marketing department

   b. It validates personal hunches about the market

   c. It transforms raw data into actionable insights

   d. It simplifies the development process for new products

3. **Which of the following is NOT directly influenced by marketing research?**

   a. Developing new product lines

   b. Leveraging brand strength

   c. Mitigating supply chain risks

   d. Addressing product dependency

4. **Real-world examples of marketing research are presented in this chapter to demonstrate its impact on**

   a. Increasing brand awareness

   b. Understanding consumer behavior

   c. Streamlining marketing budgets

   d. Improving employee training programs

5. **According to the passage, marketing research can bring about significant and lasting success in**

    a. Industries that are highly regulated

    b. Competitive markets

    c. Non-profit organizations

    d. Government agencies

6. **What is the MAIN purpose of marketing research?**

    a. To create visually appealing marketing materials

    b. To gather information for better decision-making

    c. To track competitor activity only

    d. To conduct employee satisfaction surveys

7. **Marketing research helps to**

    a. Ignore customer feedback

    b. Unravel complexities of consumer behavior

    c. Focus solely on production processes

    d. Eliminate the need for marketing campaigns

8. **The chapter likens marketing research to a "guiding light in uncertainty." What does this suggest about the business landscape?**

    a. It is a stable and predictable environment.

    b. It is constantly changing and evolving.

    c. It is easily controlled by businesses themselves.

    d. It offers limited opportunities for growth.

9. **Marketing research is said to "unravel" consumer behavior. What does this imply about consumer behavior itself?**

    a. It is always simple and straightforward.

    b. It can be complex and multifaceted.

    c. Consumers always make logical decisions.

    d. Consumer behavior is easily predictable.

10. **How does marketing research transform raw data, according to the passage?**

    a. It erases irrelevant data points.

    b. It converts data into actionable insights.

    c. It focuses solely on numerical values.

    d. It disregards qualitative information.

Answers	1 – b	2 – c	3 – c	4 – b	5 – b
	6 – b	7 – b	8 – b	9 – b	10 – b

Chapter Summary

◆ Marketing research acts as a compass for businesses, providing direction in a dynamic marketplace.

◆ It gathers, analyzes, and interprets data to unravel consumer behavior and market trends.

◆ By transforming data into insights, marketing research empowers businesses to make strategic decisions.

◆ Real-world examples demonstrate the impact of research on navigating consumer behavior complexities.

◆ These insights lead to strategic advantages like leveraging brand strengths, addressing product dependence, exploring new markets, and mitigating risks.

◆ Ultimately, marketing research plays a critical role in guiding businesses toward sustainable success in a competitive environment.

Further Reading

Refer to the following videos to enhance understanding of the concepts and examples discussed in this chapter. Links to these videos are also available in the Online Resources section of this book.

- The complete list of SurveyMonkey videos and tutorials: https://www.youtube.com/@surveymonkey

- Google Forms tutorial: https://www.youtube.com/watch?v=BtoOHhA3aPQ

- Benchmarking, types: https://www.youtube.com/watch?v=UjBy4nDeb_I

- Mystery shoppers, importance: https://www.youtube.com/watch?v=DyxY03ofGUw

- Neuromarketing, what is it? https://www.youtube.com/watch?v=1FIv6OQa6ks

- Neuromarketing, inside the mind of a consumer: https://www.youtube.com/watch?v=ZbkYV6aXdc0

Chapter **7**

The Marketing Brief and Philip Kotler's 4Ps in a Marketing Plan

This chapter focuses on strategic marketing with special consideration of the foundational elements of a marketing brief and how it is developed. We make efforts to explore the nuances of a creative brief and its impact on marketing campaigns. References are made to Philip Kotler's 4Ps Framework and how they influence marketing strategies' planning.

Key learning objectives should include the reader's understanding of the following:

- Setting the stage for strategic marketing
- Understanding the marketing brief
- The brief development process
- The creative brief
- The marketing plan and Philip Kotler's 4Ps

7.1 Understanding the Marketing Brief

It is glaring that every successful marketing campaign was crafted by utilizing a useful, well-designed marketing brief. A marketing brief can be defined as a succinct, simple, and self-explanatory document that outlines the necessary steps to be taken for executing a marketing campaign, highlighting the roles/responsibilities of those involved in the marketing, the target audience, and describing the best metrics for measuring the success of the campaign.

In the case of certain companies, such as P&G, when I worked there, the marketing brief was just one page long. Nowadays, I hesitate to recommend such a strict format when you look at the information that a marketing brief carries. Nonetheless, being efficient is a must.

A marketing brief should be considered a useful tool for crafting a successful marketing campaign because it acts as a roadmap for all the marketing team members. This helps them to fully understand the essential elements of the marketing strategy and focus on setting up marketing campaigns that will succeed.

The marketing brief, in essence, aligns an organization's business goals with its marketing processes aimed at fulfilling its target audience's needs.

In principle, consistency in messaging or value proposition is required to build a brand that is respected and patronized by consumers. By utilizing a marketing brief, an organization can deliver coherent and well-structured messaging to its target audience via various channels.

Resource allocation is a delicate balance, and the marketing brief is pivotal in ensuring efficient use. Whether budget, time, or workforce, the brief assists in judiciously distributing resources, preventing waste, and maximizing impact.

As a collaborative framework, the marketing brief fosters communication and mutual understanding among different departments. It brings everyone together on the same page, cultivating a sense of unity in the collective pursuit of campaign objectives.

Post-campaign, the marketing brief transforms into a benchmark for evaluation. The marketing team can analyze the effectiveness of the campaigns, compare their outcomes with the predetermined expectations in the initial marketing brief, and make the necessary adjustments or improvements to the marketing strategies where necessary.

Rather than just being a document, a marketing brief becomes a unified plan that ensures every aspect of a marketing campaign is properly and carefully executed. In this way, it makes it possible for the marketing team members to smoothly collaborate on all marketing initiatives.

In the context of this book on consumer behavior, the marketing brief serves as a prime example of where consumer behavior finds its place—at the core of a well-rounded target definition, influencing every strategic decision to pursue a successful campaign.

Figure 7.1 lists what an essential marketing brief includes. A more complex marketing brief will include elements portraying the whole marketing program, which we will explore later in this chapter.

| Figure 7.1 | Basic components of a marketing brief |

7.2 The Brief Development Process

Developing an effective marketing brief is the very first step in ensuring that an organization's marketing strategy is perfectly executed. This section of the book looks at some essential elements of a practical and highly useful marketing brief.

1. **Defining the purpose:**
   This entails providing a clear and understandable definition of the purpose of the marketing brief. It may also be important to highlight the expected elements that should be included while developing the brief in a way that they are aligned with the organizational objectives.

2. **Understanding the target:**
   Identifying and understanding the target audience is paramount. Demographics, behavioral patterns, attitudinal nuances, and aspirational elements provide a comprehensive view. A well-crafted target profile lays the

foundation for impactful marketing strategies. Demographic definitions are usually the least important from a strategic point of view. Do thoughtful and thorough reviews on more essential features.

3. **Crafting a positioning statement:**
   The positioning statement is the compass that directs marketing endeavors. It follows a distinct format: "To convince the (target audience summary) that (brand) is..." This statement succinctly encapsulates the unique value proposition and differentiators that set the brand apart.

4. **Understanding the reasons to believe:**
   In building credibility, reasons to believe (RTBs) are pivotal. These can be categorized into objective, subjective, and a combination of both. Objective RTBs are factual and tangible, while subjective ones tap into emotions and perceptions. A judicious blend creates a compelling case for the brand.

5. **Tagline magic:**
   With a tagline, an organization can condense a lot of meanings into a single phrase or slogan that is easy for consumers to quickly digest. For example, Starbucks' "Crafting Connections, One Sip at a Time," creates a sensational magic that the company is fully committed to ensuring that its customers enjoy coffee while maintaining good relationships with friends, colleagues, families, etc.

6. **Collaboration and best practices:**
   Effective collaboration between marketing teams and other departments is crucial. Regular communication, shared insights, and a collaborative mindset ensure the marketing brief resonates across various functions. Input from product development, sales, and customer service teams enriches the brief with diverse perspectives.

7. **Iterative refinement:**
   The brief is not static; it evolves through iterative refinement. Regular reviews, feedback loops, and

adaptability to changing market dynamics guarantee that the brief remains a dynamic and relevant guide throughout the campaign.

In conclusion, developing a marketing brief is an artful blend of strategic foresight, audience understanding, and collaborative synergy. It's a compass that guides teams through the labyrinth of marketing challenges, ensuring that every campaign is not just a creative endeavor but a purposeful step towards overarching business success.

7.2.1 Real-life examples and analysis

The following is my guess on what the original Starbucks marketing brief could have been, based on the available information. It covers all the basic components described in Figure 7.1 and will serve as an interesting example and guideline for all readers.

1. **Brand:** Starbucks Coffee

2. **Target market:**
    *   **Demographic target:**
        *   **Age:** Primarily targeting individuals aged 18 to 45, capturing young adults and established professionals
        *   **Income level:** Middle to upper-middle-class individuals with disposable income for premium coffee experiences
        *   **Occupation:** Professionals, students, and creatives seeking a comfortable environment for work or relaxation
    *   **Behavioral target:**
        *   **Lifestyle:** Individuals with an active and busy lifestyle who value convenience and appreciate on-the-go options
        *   **Frequency:** Regular coffee consumers who visit coffee shops multiple times a week

- **Tech-Savvy:** Embraces technology, using mobile apps for orders and rewards
- **Attitudinal target:**
  - **Value connection:** People who appreciate community values, sustainability, and social responsibility
  - **Quality seekers:** Those who prioritize high-quality, premium coffee and enjoy diverse and innovative flavors
  - **Experience enthusiasts:** Individuals who see coffee consumption as an experience, not just a beverage
- **Aspirational target:**
  - **Urban explorers:** This refers to individuals who place much value on the cosmopolitan lifestyle, such as those admiring the convenience of drinking coffee in the city setting.
  - **Social influencers:** They are people who choose to associate themselves with certain brands and their perceived values, reflecting the public image of prestige or sophistication.
  - **Creative minds:** This refers to a group of creative people that patronize Starbucks to work on their creative projects, deriving inspiration from the café's comfortable atmosphere.

3. **Positioning statement:**
   - "To convince coffee enthusiasts and community seekers that Starbucks is the unparalleled destination for curated coffee experiences. We offer a haven where passion, quality, and community converge, providing a personalized journey beyond coffee, creating moments that inspire and connect."

4. **Reasons to believe:**
   - **Objective reasons:**
     - **Consistent quality:** Starbucks concentrates on maintaining quality in all its cafés across the globe by ensuring only premium coffee beans are consistently processed for customers.
     - **Global reach:** Irrespective of the location where its café is situated, whether in Tokyo, London, or New York, Starbucks focuses on serving high-quality coffee that consumers like.
   - **Subjective reasons:**
     - **Community connection:** By bringing people from different races, social classes, and economic statuses together to share coffee while connecting with one another, Starbucks fosters a dynamic community for diverse individuals.
     - **Personalized experience:** Individual customers are also served uniquely at Starbucks' cafes because they can choose whatever drinks and snacks they desire with ease.
   - **Combined reasons:**
     - **Innovation in offerings:** Starbucks blends the traditional coffee service with modern, innovative offerings by providing contemporary flavors that coffee purists as well as connoisseurs can comfortably choose from and enjoy.
     - **Sustainability commitment:** Starbucks demonstrates an unwavering commitment to the conservation of the planet Earth through the ethical sourcing of its coffee and its environmentally friendly practices, in addition to providing quality coffee to consumers.

5. **Taglines**
   - **Real-life tagline:** "Inspiring and Nurturing the Human Spirit – One Person, One Cup, and One Neighborhood at a Time."

- **Our take on a more convenient tagline:** "Crafting Connections, One Sip at a Time"

This brief example will facilitate our analysis of the brief and how it should be used. Remember, it is a fundamental, unavoidable part of any solid marketing plan.

7.3 A Marketing Brief's Endless World of Sophistication

If we would like to add information to a marketing brief, we would find that each marketing-savvy firm will have its own "perfect formula." As a marketing professor and consultant, I emphasize on this every time I speak about this issue with students and clients. This is an ever-improving process, and I am glad it is so.

While attempting to demystify the marketing brief, we find some key elements that are crucial for its success. Here's a breakdown of key elements typically found in a marketing brief:

1. **Objective:**
   Clearly state the primary purpose of the marketing effort. Is it to launch a new product, increase brand awareness, or boost sales?

2. **Market Overview:**
   Competitive Landscape: Identify the differences between your brand and your main competitors and highlight your unique selling propositions (USPs). Describe what differentiates your brand from the others in the marketplace.

   Trends: Briefly discuss current industry trends that might affect consumer behavior. Understanding these trends helps tailor messages and strategies effectively.

3. **SWOT Analysis:**
   With SWOT Analysis, you can analyze your organization's internal strengths and weaknesses as well as opportunities and threats existing externally.

   Your organization's strengths could include its strong brand reputation, huge and loyal customer base, or innovative line of products/services.

   Its weaknesses may include but are not limited to a small market share, overreliance on a single market, or high pricing.

   Gaining an entry into a new market, cashing in on a new trend, or creating new products/services could be your organization's opportunities.

   However, your organization may face some external threats such as a sudden change in consumers' needs, increased competition, or economic slowdowns/downturns.

4. **Marketing objectives:**
   It is sensible to describe SMART goals (Specific, Measurable, Achievable, Relevant, and Time-bound). This action is required to be able to measure the marketing campaign's success.

   Examples of SMART goals may include improving customer relationships, increasing sales by 5-10% in the next 3-4 months, or discovering a new customer segment that will be interested in your organization's products/services.

5. **Channels and touchpoints:**
   Distinctly describe the communication channels you will be using to get in touch with your audience. This may involve using traditional communication channels like TV, radio, or print, and digital channels such as email marketing, and social media. It is equally possible to combine both traditional and digital communication tools for better outreach.

   Discover the most important touch points between your brand and your audience, and double down on creating consistent and constant messaging that will keep them updated about your organization's products/services and other activities.

6. **Core components:**
   Depending on the campaign's focus, highlight essential components such as key product features, unique selling propositions, or distinctive brand attributes. What makes your offering stand out?

7. **Implementation plan:**
   Offer a detailed overview of how the campaigns will be executed. As a roadmap, this should highlight any collaborations or partnerships that will be required in order to successfully implement your organization's marketing plan.

8. **Target audience:**
   Define a clear picture of your target audience. What are their demographics, preferences, or needs? Taking this step is very crucial for targeting the right consumer segments.

   Creating messaging that will perfectly resonate with your target audience is equally essential so as to attract their attention and stimulate loyalty in them, toward your products and services. Focus on your brand's core messages and deliver them in a way that will differentiate you from your competitors.

9. **Timeline and budget:**
   Establish a sensible timeframe for the start and completion of the campaign processes. Moreover, allot a realistic budget to cover the entire marketing campaign as well as putting aside extra resources to fund some significant marketing activities such as digital marketing, product launching, or enhancing customer experience.

10. **Success metrics:**
    Outline the key performance indicators (KPIs) that will be utilized in measuring the campaign's success. Some of the

common metrics used by organizations include web traffic, customer satisfaction scores, increased sales, and social media engagement.

Paying close attention to the KPIs can be instrumental in identifying the campaign's effectiveness and discovering areas that deserve some improvements.

11. Risks and mitigations:
Design strategies that may be used to mitigate any risks or issues that could occur during the entire campaign duration. Failure to do this might disrupt the entire marketing activity.

12. Approval:
Create a space for approval on the marketing brief, where relevant individuals can review and append their signatures, indicating that they have agreed to the marketing terms which are in line with your organization's business goals. This approach helps bring everyone on board and could engender unity while pursuing a common marketing goal.

A comprehensive and easy-to-implement marketing brief, consisting of all the above-mentioned elements, can streamline the process of setting up successful marketing campaigns. Such a brief will be used as a blueprint for achieving high-performing marketing initiatives that align with your organization's business goals.

We have three families of documents: The marketing plan, the marketing brief, and the creative brief. We are listing them in order of importance and following their strategic reach. We already discussed the marketing brief and the marketing plan will be discussed in the next section. I would like to shed some light on a creative brief here.

A creative brief follows the marketing brief structure, yet it is meant to be based on a specific tactic campaign. An example of a creative brief is provided below, for a new Starbucks coffee product named Dulce de leche Frappuccino, which is developed for coffee drinkers who love premium, international flavors.

Creative Brief: Starbucks Dulce de Leche Frappuccino Launch
- **Objective:**
  - To properly introduce Starbucks' new coffee product, Dulce de leche Frappuccino, to excite, existing customers who are already of Starbucks' quality and convenience of service.

- **Target Audience:**
  - **Primary Audience:** Those in the age range 25-40 who are urban professionals who prioritize high-quality coffee and good customer experience over traditional offerings in rundown cafés.

  - **Secondary Audience:** They are enthusiastic coffee drinkers who are aged 20-35, enjoy exploring the different flavors of coffee, and are open to experimenting with new beverages.

  - **Third-level Audience:** They are Latin coffee connoisseurs, urban, and are quite familiar with premium coffee such as Dulce de leche taste.

- **Product positioning statement:**
  - "Convince our urban professionals seeking a break from the ordinary: Starbucks Dulce de Leche Frappuccino, a sublime fusion of rich caramel and creamy sweetness, awaits to elevate your coffee experience. Indulgence Redefined."

- **Reasons to believe:**
  - **Objective:** Created by using the combination of best-in-class Arabica beans and caramel sauce that produce a premium taste.

  - **Subjective:** Starbucks' commitment to quality – blending expertise and customer feedback.

- **Campaign theme:**
  - "Indulgence Redefined"
- **Channels:**
  - **Digital platforms:** Offering short videos via Instagram stories, Facebook Live, and Teaser videos.

  - **In-Store Experience:** Using attractive table displays, interactive promotions, and in-store posters to engage customers.
- **Launch Date:**
  - 1st day of the 2nd Quarter of the fiscal year.
- **Budget:**
  - **Total Budget:** $2 million.
- **Allocation:**
  - **Digital Marketing:** $1 million.

  - **In-Store Promotions:** $500,000.

  - **Launch Event:** $500,000.
- **Success metrics:**

- **Key Performance Indicators (KPIs):**
  - 20% increase in Frappuccino sales.

  - 30% growth in social media mentions during the launch week.

  - Positive customer feedback on taste and experience.
- **Creative elements:**
  - **Visuals:** Vibrant imagery showcasing the Dulce de Leche Frappuccino.
- **Slogan:**
  - "Savor Sweet Moments."
- **Promotions:**
  - Limited-time offers and rewards for early adopters.

- **Tagline:**
  - "Savor Sweet Moments."
- **Risks and Mitigations:**
  - **Customer Resistance:** Highlight the blend's unique qualities through enticing visuals and promotions.

  - **Supply Chain Issues:** Collaborate closely with suppliers to ensure a smooth launch.
- **Approval:**
  - **Campaign Lead:** Product Marketing Manager, Starbucks
- **Date:**
  - Date of Approval

7.4 The Marketing Plan and Phillip Kotler's 4Ps

In the dynamic business landscape, the compass that guides successful marketing strategies is the marketing plan. Central to this plan is a framework that has become a cornerstone in the field of marketing – Philip Kotler's 4Ps.

Mr.Kotler is an American Economist, who studied at the University of Chicago and earned his Ph.D. at MIT. I personally had the honor of being one of his students at J.L. Kellogg School, at Northwestern University. He made significant contributions to marketing as the author of over 80 books and a consultant for renowned companies across the globe. In 2003, the Financial Times described Kotler's three contributions to marketing and to management:

Kotler's 4Ps, designed by Philip Kotler and first published in his book "Marketing Management", highlight the four primary elements every successful marketing plan should incorporate: They are product, price, place, and promotion.

1. Product

The "product" element of the 4Ps involves the product/service an organization offers to its target audience in order to meet their wants and needs. This also includes the product's design, features, branding, quality, and post-purchase services. An effective marketing plan will include the product's unique selling points and highlight its great features that can convince the target audience to patronize the product.

2. Price

Organizations often struggle with pricing their products/services because they want them to be affordable as well as being able to make enough profits from them to keep their day-to-day operations going. However, it is imperative that organizations utilize a competitive pricing strategy that will make their products/services affordable to consumers while setting aside enough funds to cover their production, marketing, and other related business activities. A good price should reflect the perceived quality of a product/service but shouldn't be too expensive for those who will be purchasing it.

3. Place

The "place" element of the 4Ps emphasizes consumers' accessibility to the product/service through effective distribution channels. While drafting a marketing plan, it is important to state where and how consumers can quickly find the product to buy it. This entails making the product available via retail outlets, partnerships, online platforms, and direct-to-consumer supply chains.

4. Promotion

The "promotion" component requires advertising the product, creating awareness about it to consumers, and encouraging them to purchase it. An organization can either choose to utilize the traditional techniques of promoting its product on TV, in print, via public relations, and sales promotions, or take advantage of digital marketing procedures such as promoting it online and through social media. Whichever approach is adopted, it is imperative that the messaging used for the marketing must be concise, powerful, and convincing enough to consumers.

7.5 Crafting an Effective Marketing Plan

Organizations need to carefully incorporate the 4Ps into their marketing processes in the following ways:

1. **Research and analysis:**
   It is helpful to have a firm understanding of the industry trends, competition, and target market before applying the 4Ps in a marketing plan. Through effective research and analysis, an organization can obtain some useful insights that can be incorporated into its place, product, price, and promotional procedures.

2. **Alignment with business objectives:**
   In practice, it is expected that the 4Ps must seamlessly align with the organization's overall business goals; this could be in the areas of creating new markets or expanding the existing market shares, creating and launching new products, and/or encouraging brand loyalty.

3. **Flexibility and adaptability:**
   An effective marketing plan must be flexible and accommodating to unforeseeable changes in the market dynamics, consumers' preferences, and emerging industry trends. In other words, the marketing must be adjustable and improvable all along the organization's marketing activities.

4. **Measurement and evaluation:**
   The key performance indicators (KPIs) are useful for measuring the success of a typical marketing plan. By regularly reviewing the KPIs, it is possible to discover areas

that require urgent improvements so as to ensure that the marketing plan is in line with the organization's long-term business objectives.

In conclusion, incorporating Kotler's 4Ps, a comprehensive framework, into its marketing plan can help an organization stay ahead of its competitors by systematically understanding the market dynamics, consumers' expectations, and changing industry trends.

Quiz

1. **What is the PRIMARY purpose of a marketing brief?**

   a. To showcase creative ideas for a marketing campaign.

   b. To serve as a roadmap for aligning marketing efforts with business goals.

   c. To provide detailed instructions for the design team.

   d. To track marketing campaign expenses.

2. **Which of these is NOT a fundamental component of a marketing brief?**

   a. Brand/product information

   b. Target market demographics

   c. Budgetary constraints

   d. Competitor analysis

3. **What real-world example is used in the passage to illustrate the components of a marketing brief?**

   a. Apple's recent iPhone launch campaign.
   (The passage may use various examples.)

   b. Starbucks' marketing strategy.
   (The passage may use various examples.)

   c. A social media marketing campaign for a new fitness app. (The passage may use various examples.)

   d. A television commercial for a car manufacturer.
   (The passage may use various examples.)

4. **How does a marketing brief necessitate an effective marketing campaign?**

    a. It provides a list of celebrities to endorse the product.

    b. It ensures consistency in messaging across all marketing channels.

    c. It serves as a platform for brainstorming creative ideas.

    d. It assigns specific tasks to individual team members.

5. **Which step in the development process of a marketing brief emphasizes understanding the target audience?**

    a. Defining the purpose of the campaign.

    b. Understanding the target audience.

    c. Crafting a catchy tagline.

    d. Identifying channels for promotion.

6. **Which of the following marketing mix frameworks is used alongside the marketing plans?**

    a. The AIDA model (Attention, Interest, Desire, Action)

    b. Philip Kotler's 4Ps (Product, Price, Place, Promotion)

    c. The Ansoff Matrix (Market Penetration, Market Development, Product Development, Diversification)

    d. The Customer Decision Journey (Awareness, Consideration, Decision, Retention)

7. **What are some important aspects of incorporating a marketing brief into a marketing plan?**

   a. Specificity about brand colors and fonts.

   b. Research, alignment with business goals, and measurement.

   c. Selecting the most visually appealing marketing materials.

   d. Focusing solely on online marketing channels.

8. **The development of a marketing brief should be:**

   a. A one-time process completed before any campaign work begins.

   b. An iterative process with opportunities for refinement.

   c. Delegated solely to the marketing department.

   d. Focused on short-term results only.

9. **The passage emphasizes a marketing brief's core benefit as:**

   a. Increased creativity.

   b. Focus on vision and direction.

   c. Faster campaign development.

   d. Lower campaign costs.

10. **How does a marketing brief ensure consistency in marketing efforts?**

    a. By suggesting a single communication channel.

    b. By outlining key messaging and brand elements.

    c. By providing a platform for open debate.

    d. By focusing on individual team member styles.

Answers	1 – b	2 – d	3 – b	4 – b	5 – b
	6 – b	7 – b	8 – b	9 – b	10 – b

Chapter Summary

◆ Marketing briefs are essential tools for aligning marketing efforts with overall business goals.

◆ They capture campaign essentials in a clear and concise document.

◆ Key components include brand information, target audience, positioning statement, reasons to believe, and tagline.

◆ The Starbucks model provides a well-structured example of a marketing brief.

◆ The benefits of using marketing briefs include focused vision, consistency across marketing efforts, optimized resource allocation, improved collaboration, and a benchmark for evaluation.

◆ The development process involves defining the campaign's purpose, understanding the target audience, crafting a positioning statement, fostering collaboration, and iterative refinement to achieve strategic alignment.

◆ Marketing briefs consider the marketing mix (Kotler's 4Ps): product, price, place, and promotion.

◆ Integration with the overall marketing plan is crucial, ensuring alignment with research, goals, and flexibility for adaptation.

◆ By establishing a cohesive strategy, marketing briefs contribute to driving business growth through a unified approach.

◆ A marketing brief serves as a roadmap to success, guiding campaign development and execution.

Further Reading

Refer to the following videos to enhance understanding of the concepts and examples discussed in this chapter. Links to these videos are also available in the Online Resources section of this book.

- Starbucks marketing strategy: https://www.youtube.com/watch?v=ijq0WVLJsnY

- Creating a marketing brief: https://www.youtube.com/watch?v=EBRJpyt-dFs

- Creating a marketing plan: https://www.youtube.com/watch?v=4ti_uK60nLk

- A plan is not a strategy: https://www.youtube.com/watch?v=iuYlGRnC7J8

- The 4Ps of the marketing plan: https://www.youtube.com/watch?v=Mco8vBAwOmA

This page is intentionally left blank

Chapter **8**

"P" Number 1: Product - Packaging From a Product's Feature Perspective

In Chapter eight, we will be focusing on the first "p", which represents "product". We will explore how product packaging plays a significant role in influencing consumer behavior. Each product packaging is designed based on the apparent feature(s) that the product has. Consumers, in general, are motivated to purchase a product depending on the product's perceived value and its attractive packaging.

Key learning objectives should include the reader's understanding of the following:

- Understanding the first "p"; a mnemotechnic rule to understand products, services, and ideas; from a marketing perspective
- Understanding the essence of a product, defining what constitutes a product in the eyes of the consumer
- Examining the lifecycle of a product
- Learning strategies to avoid product obsolescence

> • Understanding the impact of packaging on consumer behavior

8.1 Understanding the "P" for Products, Services, and Ideas

Often regarded as the Father of Modern Marketing, Philip Kotler invented the concept of the 4Ps, which he ably introduced in his 1967 popular book titled, "Marketing Management." He used the mnemonic "p" to denote "product". His concept reveals, in detail, how a product is one of the value-creation entities that can be used for consumer engagement.

The product is the first element of Kotler's framework and serves as a foundational principle for marketers worldwide. It encompasses not only physical goods but also services and ideas that fulfill customers' needs and desires. It represents the offering itself and includes tangible features, intangible attributes, and perceived benefits. Kotler's framework underscores the importance of a comprehensive understanding of products in marketing strategy development.

8.1.1 Products, services, and ideas in marketing

1. **Products:** These include physical products such as cars, items of furniture, household appliances, and cell phones. Marketers must pay attention to a product's design, features, quality, brand, and packaging when marketing it to consumers, and do so in a way that will influence their purchasing decisions.

2. **Services:** Services constitute intangible offerings such as healthcare, hospitality, and consulting. The product framework extends to services, emphasizing factors like

reliability, responsiveness, empathy, and assurance in service delivery.

3. **Ideas:** Ideas represent concepts, beliefs, or initiatives aimed at influencing behavior or fostering change. Whether promoting social causes, political campaigns, or educational programs, marketers apply the product rule to craft compelling narratives and persuasive messaging. As we expressed before, the difference between a service and an idea is that ideas are not "sold" for a price. Let me give you an example here, and some clarifications. The world of political marketing is one of the most important in terms of investment, yet candidates' ideas are not "sold" to citizens but "expressed to citizens" and they are supposed to support these ideas with their votes. I present you an idea, you like it and you vote for it. You are probably thinking that candidates frequently present money-raising campaigns in order to make their marketing programs possible and I say yes, yet this is optional. You can freely decide to give money to a candidate. Some other readers may say that they know of an app (a service) that is free and Google may be the most popular free service in the world today. Yet, Google does require you to do something in return, they collect your data. In summary, there is this definition that I wrote about and then, there are exceptions to the rule. That is what the world is like, right?

The product "p" mnemonic provides marketers with a structured approach to conceptualize and analyze offerings across diverse contexts. By considering products, services, and ideas through this framework, marketers can develop more effective strategies to meet customer needs and achieve organizational objectives.

8.2 Understanding the Essence of a Product: Defining Consumer Perception

Understanding the essence of a product is paramount. This entails delving into how consumers perceive products, encompassing tangible features, intangible attributes, and the overall value proposition. This section specifically looks at how consumers perceive the different values a product has, and how their perceptions influence their buying decisions.

The significance of a product extends beyond the fact that it is a tangible (material or physical) object that users can derive a lot of benefits from while using it; in addition to its physical qualities such as design, performance, and functionality, a product can equally serve as an object to showcase a brand image, prestige, emotional connection, status, etc., which are referred to as a product's intangible attributes.

Consumers can have different perceptions of the same product due to a number of factors; these may include but are not limited to their beliefs, cultural impacts, experiences, and social considerations. How a consumer appreciates the quality and uniqueness of a product may be connected to the way they perceive the product's durability, affordability, functionality, and whether the product meets their personal needs at that particular period in time or not.

8.2.1 Key elements of product perception

1. **Tangible features**
   Consumers assess products based on their physical characteristics, including design, color, size, and functionality. These attributes influence perceived value and usability, impacting purchasing decisions. Elaborating on this concept, we can take some examples.

- **Car quality vs car design:** Regular consumers have a harder time evaluating the real quality of a car vs the car design. They normally make assumptions about the car's quality just by looking at how the car looks. The old saying "never judge a book by its cover" was not written by any marketer. A car that looks "bulky" will have consumers believe that it will not be fast on the road, even without starting it up. So car brands look for the best designers, like Toyota opening a design center in Cote d'Azur, France to get European flavor to their models.

- **Why dentists tend to dress in white:** White will let consumers understand how clean a dentist's office is. Simple as that. White makes cleanliness tangible.

- **Vodkas tend to have clear bottles:** Examples like Ciroc, a famous French vodka, which incidentally is made of grapes, is slim, long, and crystal clear. All vodkas speak of purity. So, this bottle makes this feature tangible.

2. **Intangible attributes**
Beyond tangible features, intangible aspects such as brand reputation, perceived quality, and emotional appeal significantly influence product perception. Brands that evoke positive emotions, trust, and credibility tend to resonate more with consumers.

For example, credit cards will sell on security, the fact that if you need to pay for something you do not need to worry to bring cash with you. They can even play with the idea that there are no limits to your expenditures, which is not precisely true by the way. So freedom and security are very often attributes assigned to banking cards.

3. **Value proposition**
A product's value proposition is largely related to how useful it is, what specific problem(s) it solves, and how it meets consumers' needs or preferences. Naturally,

consumers are likely to perceive a product favorably if they can derive much benefit from using it, and it also has great features, design, and it is comparatively affordable.

Related to the value proposition, we can take ideas from some of the most recognized airlines in the US. I have to tell you that some airlines do not have the best service, yet they do have good customer ratings. According to a report from the American Customer Satisfaction Index,[6] number two on the list is the low-cost airline Southwest. As we all very well know, low cost inevitably leads to trimmed service options. Nevertheless, consumers are smart enough to understand that you get what you pay for, and sometimes more. This formula is called a "value proposition". The higher the price, the higher the expectation, this is a general rule for customer satisfaction. A good value is a positive evaluation given what you could charge for the service.

It is important for marketers to always remember that the consumers' perceptions of a product revolve around various factors, which have already been discussed in this section. In order to stimulate consumers to make buying decisions, marketers must present, as understandably as possible, the great benefits consumers stand to gain from utilizing the product. This is the right step to take in making a product stand out in a very competitive marketplace.

8.3 Product Life-Cycle

Every product goes through a unique life cycle, from the time they are introduced to the market to the time they are discontinued and removed from distribution. Businesses need to be fully aware of all these stages in a product's life cycle to

---

6 The American Customer Satisfaction Index. "Airlines." https://theacsi.org/industries/travel/airlines/.

be able to make sensible business decisions relating to product development, marketing, and the removal of the product from the supply chain. This section highlights the different stages in a product's life cycle, its intrinsic characteristics, and its overall impacts on businesses. The 4 stages of the product life cycle are elaborated in Table 8.1.

As a newly hired employee, I was once privileged to share a dinner with the CEO of P&G, the multinational manufacturer of many popular consumer products. I remember very vividly that he said that a product decline or maturity in a product's life cycle was a problem generated by "lazy" brand managers, people who did not take the time and effort to make their products shine over and over again in time. As a guideline, this is a brilliant concept and idea, and I wanted to share that lesson with all of you. P&G defines itself as an R&D company, more than a marketing company as many people recognize it to be. R&D allows P&G to have premium products in most or all categories, allowing for premium margins across most categories they operate in.

Table 8.1	Stages of the product life cycle

Stages	Characteristics	Strategic Implications
Stage 1: Introduction	• Product launched into the market • Sales typically low as awareness is built • High promotional and distribution expenses	• Focus on product differentiation to attract early adopters • Heavy marketing and promotional activities to create awareness • Limited product variations to test market response

Stages	Characteristics	Strategic Implications
Stage 2: Growth	• A rapid increase in sales and market acceptance • Competitors enter the market, leading to increased competition • Product improvements and expanded distribution channels	• Capitalize on market acceptance and expand market share • Enhance product features and quality to maintain competitiveness • Invest in distribution channels and expand market reach
Stage 3: Maturity	• Sales growth stabilizes, reaching peak levels • Market saturation leads to intense competition and price pressures • Focus on cost reduction and efficiency	• Differentiate the product to maintain market share • Cut costs to sustain profitability amidst price pressures • Explore new market segments or product variations to extend the product's lifecycle
Stage 4: Decline	• Sales decline due to changing consumer preferences or technological advancements • Profits diminish, and resources may be reallocated to other products • Market consolidation as weaker competitors exit the market	• Evaluate options such as product redesign, repositioning, or discontinuation • Manage the decline phase effectively to maximize profits or salvage the remaining market share • Consider diversification or innovation to replace declining product revenue

8.3.1 Key considerations for businesses

Product life cycle is a critical aspect of a marketing campaign since there are some general guidelines that are common to stages and these are worth taking a look at. I normally say "The model is no model, just think!" But these "models" are a nice guideline for thoughtful thinking. Following are some key considerations for businesses based on the product life cycle:

1. **Market monitoring:**
    -   Continuous monitoring of market trends and consumer preferences
    -   Early identification of life cycle stages to facilitate timely strategic adjustments

2. **Strategic planning:**
    -   Formulation of strategies tailored to each lifecycle stage
    -   Flexibility to adapt strategies based on market dynamics and competitive pressures

3. **Resource allocation:**
    -   Allocation of resources based on lifecycle stage priorities
    -   Investment in innovation and new product development to sustain long-term growth

4. **Customer relationship management:**
    -   Maintenance of customer relationships throughout the lifecycle
    -   Strategies to retain loyal customers and attract new ones at different stages

In summary, by having deep knowledge of their product's life cycles, businesses can strategically manage each stage of their product's trajectories, from their introduction to the market to their decline, and maximize opportunities while their products are still reigning in the ever-competitive markets.

8.3.2 Industry examples

1. **Introduction stage:**
    If you look at products in the infancy stage, we can think of Starlink, Elon Musk's creation to deliver internet across

the globe directly from privately owned satellites. Musk believes that there is a market of people around the world that does not want or cannot receive cable-based services or cellphone network services. Starlink charges a premium for its service, yet you can have internet basically anywhere on planet Earth. As a new product, it follows the traditional model of high introduction costs, heavy advertisement requirements (compared to sales), premium price, and search for unique target markets, among others.

2. **Growth stage:**

   A growing product is Hoka One One, a brand that I am a fan of. Hoka is the brainchild of former Salomon executive, Jean Luc Diard from France. He and colleague Nicolas Mermoud thought that there was a not-well-served market of shoes out there for over-40-year-old runners. They developed a new shoe with maximum cushioning, so tall that when I personally wore it the first time, my gym friends called me Mr.Ronald McDonalds! In any case, Hoka is growing its market share in the competitive running market with nothing less than highly cushioned sports shoes. [7] They have grown to 8.7% from 4.2% in 2023. As a growing brand, some natural conclusions are, that they have high advertising expenditures (yet lower than the introduction stage on a dollar sales basis), growing marketing channels base, product diversification, and high margins, among other typical situations.

3. **Maturity stage:**

   A mature product is, by contrast, the regular running shoe by Nike or Adidas. This does not mean that they are not selling and investing in new products! But their lion's share of their business is on simple, reliable running shoes. Typical situations are a lower price range, lower per-sales

---

7 Rajesh, Ananya Mariam, and Ananya Mariam Rajesh. "Federer-Backed On, Decker's Hoka Starting to Take More Retail Shelf Space from Nike, Adidas." *Reuters*, November 29, 2023, sec. Retail & Consumer. https://www.reuters.com

dollar advertising expenditures, and massive marketing channels, among other typical situations.

4. **Decline stage:**
   Finally, the hard example to give is a declining product category. One of the classic examples is the Blackberry phone, which is no longer with us on the planet. It was an outstanding product that did not live up to the iPhone and Android competition and consumer demand. Currently, they are almost nonexistent in the market, but in their final years, they were a declining product. [8]

8.4 Strategies to Avoid Product Obsolescence From a Consumer Behavior Perspective

As the P&G story I mentioned earlier said, a mature and declining product is the result of lazy brand managers, here is a list of alternative ways to improve your product performance in time.

From the standpoint of consumer behavior, the best approach for preventing a product from becoming obsolete is to fully understand and quickly adapt to consumers' changing preferences, market trends, and innovations. The following strategies can be utilized to prevent product obsolescence:

1. **Continuous market research:**
   I believe that marketing is a process, and as such, a control point is vital. This point will make it possible for you to create new strategies or refine your existing ones. You can carry out consistent market research so as to remain updated with emerging consumer trends and preferences, technological advancements, and market dynamics. For

---

8 Maiorca, Danny. "The 3 Reasons BlackBerry Failed Spectacularly—and Why They Might Rise Again." MUO, August 18, 2021. https://www.makeuseof.com

market research, you can utilize focus groups, social media, surveys, and other data-gathering tools so as to obtain insights about consumers' current behaviors.

2. **Customer feedback and engagement:**
   Customer feedback is a vital part of marketing research. It is separated just because it is not a one-shot deal but an ongoing process. With the technology now available, you cannot not take this step. You should consistently ask customers to share their pain points, needs, and preferences with you. This can be done by using surveys, feedback forms, or reviews. Platforms such as social media and online forums can be utilized to engage customers in a community-like format so as to obtain real-time information from them about your products and services.

3. **Product innovation and iteration:**
   An innovative company heavily invests in R&D, because research and development are the backbone of successful companies that regularly use their customers' feedback and data about market trends to timely improve and refine their products and services. It is equally important for businesses to adopt agile product development techniques so that they can quickly refine or update their products when necessary.

4. **Customization and personalization:**
   It is sensible to offer products and services that customers can customize and/or personalize for their individual preferences. Taking advantage of data and consumer segmentation insights, businesses can target a particular consumer segment with messaging and products that will interest them.

5. **Sustainability and ethical practices:**
   The best approach for businesses to win the trust and patronage of environmentally and socially responsible consumers is to embrace ethical practices and sustainable initiatives in their operations. Modern-day consumers

appreciate and are loyal to companies that communicate transparently with them about the sourcing of their products' raw materials, manufacturing, and sustainability procedures.

6. **Long-term relationship building:**
Build long-term and mutually beneficial relationships with your customers by offering them great loyalty programs, excellent customer service, and rewards. Pay serious attention to customer retention and satisfaction so as to encourage repeat orders of your products. Happy customers are infographic also very good at giving word-of-mouth recommendations about products/services they are satisfied with.

7. **Flexibility and adaptability:**
It is imperative that businesses remain flexible and adjustable to the changes in the market, technologies, and consumer preferences. Anticipating what future trends will look like and properly adapting to concurrent changes are the surest approaches for businesses to stay relevant and ahead of their competitors.

8. **Brand storytelling and emotional connection:**
The brand story should be compelling enough to create an emotional impact in the consumers' minds. When a brand narrative is effectively communicated to consumers, it will cause them to be emotionally connected to the brand and give them memorable experiences while using the product/ service.

| Figure 8.1 | **Strategies to avoid product obsolescence** |

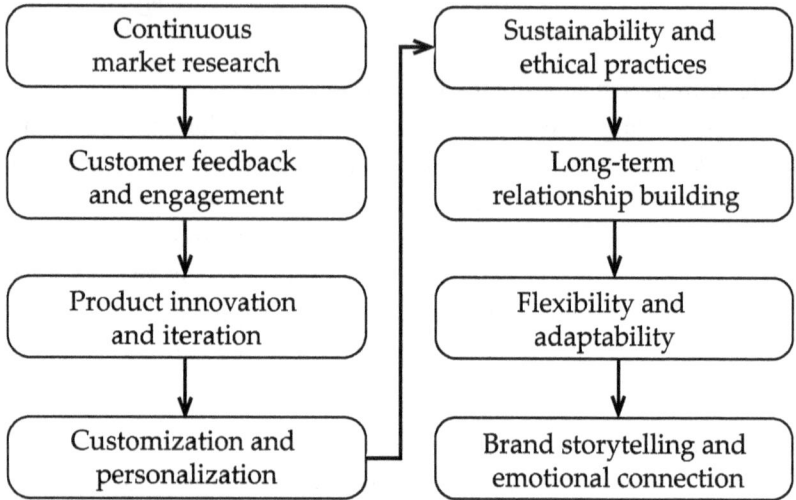

```
┌─────────────────────┐        ┌─────────────────────┐
│     Continuous      │───────▶│  Sustainability and │
│   market research   │        │   ethical practices │
└─────────────────────┘        └─────────────────────┘
          │                              │
          ▼                              ▼
┌─────────────────────┐        ┌─────────────────────┐
│  Customer feedback  │        │      Long-term      │
│   and engagement    │        │ relationship building│
└─────────────────────┘        └─────────────────────┘
          │                              │
          ▼                              ▼
┌─────────────────────┐        ┌─────────────────────┐
│  Product innovation │        │    Flexibility and  │
│    and iteration    │        │     adaptability    │
└─────────────────────┘        └─────────────────────┘
          │                              │
          ▼                              ▼
┌─────────────────────┐        ┌─────────────────────┐
│  Customization and  │───────▶│ Brand storytelling and│
│   personalization   │        │ emotional connection │
└─────────────────────┘        └─────────────────────┘
```

The above-mentioned strategies are required for businesses that want to avoid product obsolescence and steadfastly remain a leader in an ever-competitive and dynamic marketplace.

8.4.1 Industry examples

The real-life examples below are meant to illustrate the points highlighted above:

Arc'teryx and Patagonia, both specialty sporting goods and apparel businesses, are the two main companies that perfectly demonstrate that businesses can leverage market research and consumers' feedback to guard their product development and marketing initiatives.

1. **Arc'teryx:**

   - **Market research:** Arc'teryx is specifically known for using insights from its regular market research and consumers' feedback to innovate its products' design so as to increase their performance. This practice of

data-driven product development sees Arc'teryx utilize
vital information provided by a host of its customers
including climbers, hikers, skiers, and outdoor
enthusiasts to build products that are comparatively
functional and good.

- **Customer feedback and engagement:** Arc'teryx
establishes an effective feedback loop by fostering a
genuine connection with its community of customers
via social media, brand events, and online forums.
By actively requesting feedback from its customers,
Arc'teryx has been able to use that useful information
to improve its product designs in a way that meets
customers' expectations and preferences.

2. **Patagonia:**
- **Market research:** As a company that prides itself
on practices that are environmentally and socially
acceptable, Patagonia continues to conduct market
research on these two intrinsic values consumers
usually associate with its operations. Patagonia
undertakes research on consumers' perspectives on
sustainability and makes products that satisfy those
customer segments who are constantly yearning
for products that are environmentally friendly and
ethical.

- **Customer feedback and engagement:** The most
effective approach Patagonia has been using to
build and maintain a strong connection with its
community of customers is to align its business
values of sustainability and environmental
friendliness with its customers. By participating
in related outdoor events and environmental
activism, Patagonia stays glued to its customers
while constantly asking for their opinions and

feedback through its website, social media, and other customer service channels.

There is a myriad of interesting examples explaining how popular brands have used the above-explained strategies to avoid product obsolescence. In terms of product customization and innovation, I think I prefer Nespresso's and Helix's approach. Regarding long-term customer relations, sustainability, and ethical practices, I am choosing Lexus and Starbucks. Harley Davidson and Nintendo are the best examples of incorporating flexibility and adaptability, as well as brand storytelling and emotional connections.

Refer to the Online Resources section of the book to read the detailed explanation of all these approaches.

8.5 The Impact of Packaging on Consumer Behavior

Packaging is the outer container of a product. It can be part of the product itself, allowing for its protection, or simply act as a communication media, or both. If a product does not have packaging, like cars or credit cards, the "look and feel" remains in the product itself, remember that. Finally, some services communicate part of their positioning through design, such as logos and advertisements, like a bank would do with their branches and policies.

I like to think that the word packaging also applies to all design features that communicate part of the positioning of a product or service. Remember, the best chocolates deserve the best possible box. Otherwise, how are we going to know the chocolate quality through our eyes?

It is a fact that packaging does exert an appreciable influence on consumers' purchasing behavior, brand recognition, and brand experiences. The following points demonstrate how much impact packaging has on consumer behaviors.

1. **Perception and attention:**

   • The first thing every consumer perceives about a product and its brand reputation is the packaging. If the packaging is attractive, it can communicate great value and immediately draw consumers' attention.

   • In addition to quickly catching consumers' attention, visually appealing, colorful, or well-shaped packaging can differentiate a product from others on the same shelf.

   • Packages that are well-designed evoke the impression (to consumers) that the product is of unique value, authentic, and of high quality, and consumers can be influenced by that to interact with the product.

2. **Brand Image and recognition:**

   • Packaging reflects a brand's values and identity, and it can also be used to emphasize a brand's personality traits if all the brand's products are uniformly carrying the same packaging designs or types.

   • Using premium packaging materials like embossed logos, elegant boxes, and luxury finishes can transmit some sensible information to consumers. They can decode that such a product is of premium quality, and it may be expensive, highly exclusive, and sophisticated.

   • Utilizing eco-friendly packaging materials and sustainable packaging solutions can highlight a brand's environmentally friendly reputation and resonate with consumers who are equally passionate about the same cause of protecting the environment.

3. **Information and communication:**

   • Packaging can be regarded as a viable communication tool because consumers can basically read about a product's usage, benefits, and user instructions from its packaging.

- Specific labeling helps consumers make informed choices that would meet their particular needs and preferences, using pieces of information such as product names, certifications (for example, organic, etc.), and ingredients.

- Brand storytelling can be achieved through a creative packaging design and messaging in a way that resonates emotionally with consumers and causes them to take decisive actions or even participate in exchanging brand stories, events, and product narratives with their friends and colleagues.

4. **Influence on purchase decisions:**
   - Great packaging can evoke or trigger desires and emotions in consumers and cause them to make purchasing decisions about a product they believe will meet their preferential or emotional needs.

   - Packaging that strongly appeals to consumers' needs, desires, and lifestyles can motivate them to engage in impulse buying or even switch from one brand to another.

   - Some packaging elements like promotional sales, product placements, and offerings in different sizes can impact consumers' perception of a product's value and affordability, encouraging them to purchase such a product.

5. **User experience and convenience:**
   - Packaging design can enhance user experience in relation to how portable and useful the product is, and how conveniently it can be stored.

   - Some packaging features like resealable closures, ergonomic shapes, and easily opened seals are motivating factors that can influence consumers' satisfaction and continued patronage.

- Packaging designed for people with busy lifestyles should be usable on the go, and it can equally be in a single-service format so as to give consumers some flexibility and convenience.

In conclusion, packaging does play a vital role in maximizing consumers' experience, from helping them perceive and recognize the uniqueness of a product to making purchase decisions and actually enjoying the product. Understanding this aspect of consumer behavior, businesses can use their packaging designs, messaging, and materials to create powerful narratives that can drive awareness, and boost their brand reputation and sales.

Pringles and Absolut Vodka are two examples of how packaging impacts customer satisfaction and sales. Refer to the Online Resources section of the book to learn exactly how these brands stand out with their packaging.

Quiz

1. **According to Philip Kotler's marketing mix framework, which element serves as the foundation?**
   a. Price
   b. Product
   c. Promotion
   d. Place

2. **What does the "Product" in the marketing mix encompass?**
   a. Physical goods only.
   b. Physical goods, services, and ideas.
   c. Intangible attributes only.
   d. Brand image and messaging.

3. **Effective marketing strategies for products consider:**
   a. Production costs alone.
   b. Tangible features, intangible attributes, and perceived benefits.
   c. Distribution channels only.
   d. Promotional messages solely.

4. **Which statement best describes the essence of a product?**
   a. A physical object with a specific price tag.
   b. A bundle of benefits, experiences, and associations.
   c. A marketing campaign promoting its features.
   d. The location where it is sold.

5. **What factors influence consumer perception of a product?**

    a. Advertising messages only.

    b. Tangible features, intangible attributes, and value propositions.

    c. Availability in retail stores.

    d. Celebrity endorsements.

6. **The product life cycle includes which stages?**

    a. Introduction, decline, only.

    b. Introduction, growth, maturity, decline.

    c. Research and development, launch, and sales.

    d. Branding, promotion, and distribution.

7. **What marketing strategies help avoid product obsolescence based on consumer behavior?**

    a. Focusing on short-term sales goals.

    b. Continuous market research, customer feedback, and product innovation.

    c. Reducing advertising budgets.

    d. Limiting product customization options.

8. **Philip Kotler's 4Ps framework positions the product as the "foundational element" of marketing. Why might this be the case?**

    a. Products are the most visible aspect of a brand to consumers.

    b. Products directly fulfill consumer needs and wants.

    c. Products are the easiest element to control within the marketing mix.

    d. Products require less marketing effort compared to other elements.

9. According to the passage, the concept of "product" goes "beyond physical goods." What does this imply?

    a. Only physical products require marketing strategies.

    b. Products can also be services or even intangible ideas.

    c. The physical appearance of a product is the most important factor.

    d. Consumers only care about the tangible features of a product.

10. When creating marketing strategies, what does "considering the context" in which a product is offered refer to?

    a. The materials used to manufacture the product.

    b. The target audience and how they use the product.

    c. The location where the product is displayed in a store.

    d. The price point at which the product is sold.

Answers	1 – b	2 – b	3 – b	4 – b	5 – b
	6 – b	7 – b	8 – b	9 – b	10 – b

Chapter Summary

◆ Kotler's 4Ps framework puts "product" at the center of all businesses' marketing activities.

◆ By extension, in addition to being physical goods, a product can include intangibles such as services and creative ideas.

◆ For an effective marketing process to occur, a product must be considered from the standpoint of its apparent benefits to consumers, its features, and the purpose for which it is offered or sold.

◆ It is a fact that products offer users or consumers a combination of experiences, benefits, and connections.

◆ Consumers are generally motivated to make their purchasing decisions after considering both the tangible and intangible attributes of a product.

◆ It is essential that businesses strategically approach their products' life cycles (introduction, growth, maturity, and decline) in order to maximize profitability.

◆ To successfully manage a product's life cycle, it is important for businesses to engage in market research, undertake strategic planning, and properly manage the allocation of their scarce resources.

◆ A product can be prevented from becoming obsolete in the market if its manufacturer constantly receives helpful feedback from consumers, innovates the product, and maintains a good relationship with its customers.

◆ It is necessary to demonstrate excellence in product strategy as shown by companies like Starbucks, Nespresso, Arc'teryx, and Harley-Davidson have shown.

◆ Packaging serves as a communication tool, conveying brand identity and product information.

Chapter **9**

"P" Number 2:
Price - A Customer Behavior
Perspective

Chapter nine introduces an analysis of the second
P in a marketing plan, i.e. price, from a consumer
behavior perspective. This chapter reveals the close
relationship between pricing strategies and consumer
behavior, highlighting how consumers psychologically
respond to pricing. We will also be looking critically at how
businesses can use effective pricing strategies to influence
consumers' behavior and positively impact their perceptions
of their products/services to increase profitability.

Key learning objectives should include the reader's
understanding of the following:

- Price perception
- Psychological pricing strategies
- The role of price-quality perception
- Price elasticity and demand
- Insights into irrational pricing decisions and biases
- Adapting prices to consumer behavior and market
  dynamics

> - The influence of price promotions and discounts on consumer behavior

9.1 Understanding Price Perception

Pricing is a crucial aspect of any company's business strategy. This chapter delves into how consumers, based on their individual cognitive biases, socio-economic statuses, and emotional triggers respond to prices. These psychological factors play a significant role in the way consumers judge a product's price and make purchasing decisions. Therefore, the relationship between businesses and their customers goes beyond transactional interactions—i.e. just exchange of goods and money—it largely depends on how consumers perceive the intrinsic value in each product's/service's pricing.

It is very important to stress that prices and consumer behavior are not a simple model, it is definitely not a 100% rational process. How and why consumers react to a price is a multifactorial process, which is exactly what we will delve into in this chapter.

9.1.1 Understanding the psychology of price perception

Price perception is not solely determined by objective factors such as production costs or competitive benchmarks; rather, it is deeply hidden in the human psyche. Research in behavioral economics has revealed a myriad of cognitive biases that influence how individuals evaluate prices. From anchoring bias, where consumers use initial price points as reference benchmarks, to framing effects, where the context in which prices are presented alters perceptions, these biases subtly shape consumers' willingness to pay. Anchoring bias is a situation where the consumer receives information about an initial price and "anchors" any subsequent decision on that piece of information. For example, retailers show a large price, a higher one, and one with the word "sale" on it. Consumers then think that there is a good deal, given the large, "anchor" price. Framing effect, on the other side, is how pricing information is presented to consumers to lure them into thinking that they are in front of a great deal. For example, when sites present a price with a note saying that it will be available just for that day.

Moreover, emotions play a profound role in price perception, with feelings of fairness, trust, and perceived value heavily influencing purchasing decisions. Brands that effectively tap into these emotional triggers can command premium prices and foster long-term customer loyalty. Additionally, social factors such as social proof, prestige, and status signaling can amplify price perceptions, as consumers often use prices as signals of quality, exclusivity, or social standing.

9.1.2 Strategies for optimizing price perception

In light of the intricate interplay between pricing and consumer psychology, businesses must adopt smart pricing strategies to maximize perceived value and drive purchase intent. Here are some key strategies to consider:

1. **Value-based pricing:** Instead of focusing entirely on cost-based pricing, companies can concentrate on highlighting the intrinsic values, benefits, and outcomes that consumers stand to gain by using their products/services. In this way, they can easily justify their prices, even though they may be high, and encourage consumers to appreciate the perceived value of their products/services. One example is how Microsoft prices its Office package. Today it is sold online at USD 99.99 for one year. As an alternative, consumers can use the Google Drive package, which is free. How did Microsoft come up with this price? Since it is downloadable, there is virtually no direct cost associated with one sale! Price is based on what Microsoft has defined as the value

consumers place on their products and that has been a massively successful strategy.

2. **Pricing psychology tactics:** Businesses can incorporate psychology in their pricing strategies. A couple of examples of pricing psychological tactics include charm pricing, a type of odd-even pricing, and decoy pricing. Charm pricing is when a business prices its product for $0.99 instead of $10. Decoy pricing involves displaying a slightly inferior product beside the main product. In both approaches, consumers may assume that the pricing is fair and considerate enough. These strategies will be described in further detail in section 9.2.

3. **Transparent pricing communication:** Businesses should be straightforward and honest to their customers about their pricing; it is usually difficult for companies to maintain customers' trust and loyalty if they engage in deceptive pricing that charges or overcharges consumers some hidden fees. From the onset, consumers should be fully aware of the exact amount they will be paying for a product; this entails that businesses should offer a clear and understandable breakdown of all the fees, value-added services, and costs related to a certain product.

4. **Personalized pricing strategies:** Businesses should take advantage of personalizing their pricing to increase revenue and customer satisfaction by offering fair and value-based prices to different consumer segments based on their unique behaviors, purchasing patterns, and capabilities to be able to afford such prices. Nowadays, it is possible to rely on pricing algorithms that can precisely offer prices to consumers compatible with seasonal changes, demographics, and market or industry trends.

9.2 Psychological Pricing Strategies

Businesses can utilize the concept of psychological pricing to achieve a lot of things, such as enhancing consumers' perception of their products' inherent values as well as influencing their purchasing decisions to increase sales and maximize profits. Consumer psychology, in part, reveals the kinds of cognitive biases that drive consumers' buying decisions, and businesses can utilize their knowledge of their customers' psychology to improve their revenue growth. This section takes a critical look at consumer psychology and its underlying principles and explains, in detail, how businesses can use the insights from psychological pricing to stay ahead in their respective industries.

9.2.1 Psychological concepts to consider

1. **Price-quantity effect:** The concept of price-quantity effect lies in the assumption that consumers sometimes believe that large quantities of a certain product justify its price tag, even if the product's unit price is the same or a little higher. With this realization, businesses should take advantage of this idea to offer products in bundles or bulk, with a discount, persuading consumers to show an appreciable interest in purchasing them.

2. **Decoy effect:** Businesses capitalize on the decoy effect to influence consumers' choices by introducing a third, less appealing option in a product line to persuade consumers to select the first option, even though it may be more expensive and doesn't look appealing in the first instance to consumers. Decoy products are usually offered in pricing tiers, making it possible for businesses to increase their revenue and profit.

3. **Odd-even pricing:** The tactic of giving a product a $9.99 price tag instead of $10 is referred to as the odd-even

pricing. By dropping a product's last digit by a cent, consumers may assume that they could save some money on a product that costs them $9.99 rather than $10. Businesses can cash in on a sudden increase in sales as consumers rush the product they believe has been cheaply priced.

4. **Price bundling:** With this approach, businesses can combine different products/services together and sell them as discounted bundles to consumers. The excitement that comes with paying less for a bundle than for each unit included in the package often sparks a shopping spree on the consumers' part. Most importantly, those consumers who prefer convenience and are mainly concerned about saving costs will like a deal like this.

9.2.2 Implementation and best practices

The following are some guidelines for implementing psychologically structured prices into your business:

1. **Know your target audience:** It is imperative that businesses fully understand the preferences, purchasing patterns, and demographics of their target audience. This is essential for creating effective psychological pricing that will resonate with them, causing them to spend their hard-earned money on the products/services on offer.

2. **Test and iterate:** For the fact that consumers respond differently to diverse psychological pricing tactics, it is advisable for businesses to experiment with different approaches. By undertaking A/B testing on prices and studying consumers' different reactions to them, it would be possible for businesses to identify which pricing regime will be the most effective for the target market or audience, causing consumers to make quick purchasing decisions.

3. **Create a sense of urgency:** One of the practical methods for creating a sense of urgency about a certain product is for

companies to organize time-limited offers, promotions, and flash sales. In principle, scarcity, and urgency can encourage even the most reluctant consumers to buy a product they wouldn't have bought in the first instance.

4. **Transparent pricing communication:** In addition to employing psychological pricing tactics, it is equally important that businesses communicate transparently and truthfully with their customers. It is improper to lie to or mislead consumers through sharp and deceptive practices. Such misdemeanors may have a negative effect on brand reputation as well as create an aura of distrust between businesses and their customers.

It is clear from the facts stated above that psychological pricing tactics do have some great benefits for businesses, such as increasing sales, maximizing profitability, and achieving customer satisfaction. However, these tactics should be utilized ethically, transparently, and truthfully.

9.3 The Role of Price-Quality Perception

This section of the book explores the connection between the price of a product and its perceived value, as far as consumers are concerned. Based on the price of a product, consumers can instinctively evaluate its quality, usefulness, and inherent benefits. Businesses can use their knowledge of the close relationship between price and value perception to drive sales and serve their customers satisfactorily.

9.3.1 Factors influencing price-quality perception

1. **Brand reputation:** Well-known and reputable brands tend to put a high price tag on their products, giving consumers the impression that their products are of the highest quality. For

example, BMW, Tag Heuer, and Samsung have one thing in common—they make consumers assume that the premium prices they place on their products are direct indications of prestige, comfort, luxury, and good quality that consumers stand to enjoy by utilizing their products.

2. **Product attributes:** Consumers evaluate product attributes such as design, materials, and features to gauge their quality relative to price. Products with premium features or innovative technology may justify higher price points, enhancing perceptions of quality and value. This is the case of Alfa Romeo, an Italian brand of cars whose design features and prestigious history allows them to charge premium prices for their products.

3. **Social influences:** Social factors, such as peer recommendations, expert reviews, and social proof, can influence consumers' perceptions of quality. Positive word-of-mouth and endorsements from trusted sources can enhance perceptions of value and justify higher price points. When a brand is supported by sports legend Lionel Messi, his simple indirect recommendation of him as a user makes sales increase considerably. A few weeks before this book was written, Messi acquired an unknown brand of barbecue grills for himself. The news spread and the brand saw sales skyrocket around the world!

4. **High price as an indicator of quality:** There are categories where consumers have trouble identifying quality. This is the case with wines and spirits. A high price with its correlated packaging look, will make consumers understand that they are buying a quality product in spite of the fact that they may not be able to certify that for themselves.

5. **Communication and branding:** Effective communication strategies are vital for shaping price-quality perceptions. Businesses should emphasize product attributes, unique selling propositions, and value-added benefits to justify price points and build trust with consumers.

9.4 Price Elasticity and Demand

Price elasticity of demand is one of the important concepts in economics, and it underlines how consumers' demand changes in relation to price variations. Price elasticity of demand refers to the measure of how the quantity demanded of a good or service responds to a change in its price. Specifically, it indicates the percentage change in quantity demanded resulting from a one percent change in price. A high price elasticity means that consumers are sensitive to price changes, while a low price elasticity suggests that demand is relatively inelastic, meaning consumers will continue to purchase the product even if prices rise.[9]

Since the price elasticity of demand is all about measuring consumers' responsiveness to changes in products' prices, businesses can accurately speculate or predict the fluctuations in demand for their products as they raise or lower their products' prices to maximize profitability.Businesses can leverage their understanding of the price elasticity of demand to identify the market dynamics and ever-changing consumer preferences with the view to offering prices that consumers will be willing to pay for. If done efficiently, businesses can strategically increase their revenues and profitability.

9.4.1 Factors affecting price elasticity

1. **Availability of substitutes:** Two products that are direct substitutes of each other can be best used to illustrate the principle of price elasticity of demand. For example, chicken and beef are considered substitutes, which indicates that when the price of chicken increases, there will be a corresponding elasticity in the demand for beef, because

---

9 Mankiw, N. Gregory. *Principles of Economics.* 8th ed. Boston: Cengage Learning, 2020.

consumers will automatically switch to buying beef to obtain their meat-based protein.

2. **Necessity vs. luxury goods:** In terms of price elasticity of demand, necessity goods like food and hygiene products show lower price elasticity because consumers need them irrespective of the changes in their prices. On the other hand, luxury goods like designer clothes and Rolex watches exhibit higher price elasticity in the sense that if their prices are hiked, consumers can choose to ignore them, postpone using them for a while, or even switch them to other lower-priced alternatives or substitutes.

3. **Time horizon:** Time horizon plays a significant role in determining the price elasticity of a product. When consumers are newly introduced to a product, the demand for it may be comparatively inelastic as consumers need time to fully enjoy the product's benefits or find usable alternatives/substitutes. However, over time, the demand for the same product may become more elastic as consumers respond to the sharp change in its price and exercise their flexibility in utilizing alternative products. A typical example of this narrative can be seen in a consumer who has already paid for a tour package. Even if the exchange rates suddenly go up, the consumer will still go ahead on his/her trip, having already paid for it. However, the same consumer may opt out of such a tour knowing fully that the higher exchange rates indicate that he/she will be spending more than necessary on the trip.

4. **Brand loyalty:** Brand loyalty can prevent consumers from reacting unfavorably to changes in products' prices. This entails that when consumers truly like a product because of its great quality and premium value, they will still prefer to stick to the same product even if its price goes up, leading to lower elasticity of demand for the product. Brands like Coca-Cola and family-themed bars and restaurants command a high degree of brand loyalty.

9.5 Insights into Irrational Pricing Decisions and Biases

It is evident that consumer behaviors towards products' prices are sometimes influenced by a number of biases. These biases often elicit irrational purchasing decisions from consumers. Understanding the different types of biases consumers exhibit can equip businesses with the right amount of information that they can utilize in their pricing strategies so as to maximize sales, customer satisfaction, and profitability.

9.5.1 Biases in pricing decisions

1. **Loss aversion:** Sometimes consumers are afraid of losing their hard-earned money on a product that may turn out to be valueless and useless. In other words, they won't, first of all, think about the possible things they can gain from using a new product, since they have never utilized it before. To allay such dreadful fear of loss, businesses can offer incentives such as money-backed guarantees or free trials that could encourage consumers to purchase their new products. Anytime Korean brands enter an untested, competitive market, they are always confronted with the issue that consumers might fearfully consider their low-priced products as inferior. Kia then offered a 5-years quality warranty to offset that fear. I frequently think of a product that presents this issue in a very personal and frequent fashion. That is the world of personal care products, like deodorants, antiperspirants, and feminine care products. Would you save a few dimes and risk body odor all day? What do you think the answer is?

2. **Image pricing:** Consumers frequently buy products to present an image of themself among peers. I have already talked about the "Jones' effect" in a previous chapter. This is clearly the case with some champaigns, wines, and

perfumes, among a myriad of products where consumers show off about their personalities and success.

3. **Habit purchasing:** Some consumers buy products or services out of simple habits. They have a hard time even thinking about changing brands simply because they are used to these brands. Such is the case of older and lower educated consumers, normally much more reluctant to change products or brands.

9.6 Adapting Prices to Consumer Behavior and Market Dynamics

Businesses can optimize growth and remain competitive in their respective industries if they embrace flexibility in their pricing strategies. This requires that they utilize insights drawn from data and market research to offer flexible prices that consumers can afford based on their purchasing behaviors, preferences, and market trends.

1. **Segmentation and personalization:** To increase customer satisfaction and expand their market coverage, businesses should offer specific prices that the market segments they are serving can afford. It is imperative for businesses to understand the spending power of their customers' demographics and personalize their pricing strategies in a way that creates uniform product/service accessibility to their consumers that cut across all ages, socio-economic statuses, educational levels, etc.

   This is the pivotal point in marketing, and targeting. This is so, because we have a basic, underlying assumption, that there is a group of consumers that deserves a specific offer and that for that, they are ready to pay a premium or become more loyal in the short term at least. Accor, with an extensive family of hotels like Novotel, Sofitel, and Ibis, among others, they are trying to fit consumer preferences with different choices and options.

2. **Competitive pricing analysis:** Monitoring competitors' pricing strategies provides valuable insights into how related products/services are priced in the market. Businesses can take advantage of the price differential between them and their rivals to offer competitive and affordable prices that consumers will be willing to pay for their products/services. This price optimization approach can only be successfully achieved by conducting in-depth market pricing research.

3. **Dynamic pricing strategies:** The concept of dynamic pricing enables businesses to automate their pricing strategies so that they can dynamically respond to changes in consumer preferences, fluctuations in demand, and inventory levels, and proactively checkmate their competitors' pricing actions. Using pricing algorithms can help businesses identify strategic opportunities in the market so as to maximize revenue in an ever-changing marketplace.
For example, Uber doesn't operate like other traditional taxis that charge fares based on day-time and night-time, distance, or waiting time. Instead, Uber settles for a dynamic pricing strategy that is based on demand, offering cheaper fares during low-demand periods and higher fares at peak times. Airlines, hotels, car rentals, and other services use this dynamic pricing model via their digital platforms.

4. **Utilizing advanced analytics:** Advanced analytics such as predictive analytics and machine learning algorithms can be adopted by businesses to understand some possible changes in consumer behaviors, spending patterns, and market conditions. The datasets obtained from these kinds of analytics can be utilized in making pricing decisions and for precisely speculating how consumer trends will change over time, giving businesses the chance to adjust their prices in tandem with the changes in the marketplace. Amazon has been able to offer prices based on each consumer's

information gathered by his/her navigational pattern. If you are looking for a product and you haven't placed an order in a few days, the system is ready to offer you a specific promotion to speed up your decision process.

5. **A/B testing and experimentation:** By undertaking A/B pricing testing and experimentation, businesses can carefully study the effects of price changes on consumer behaviors under certain conditions. Knowing how consumers respond to various pricing strategies in different circumstances, businesses can double down on the best outcomes and utilize the knowledge gained from the experimentation to optimize their pricing models. Airbnb, for example, employs A/B pricing testing to maximize the benefits accruable from its different listing prices. Therefore, Airbnb hosts remain competitive by taking some factors into consideration while settling on their final listing pricing, such as minimum days of stay, nightly rates, cleaning charges, rate of occupancy, and other utility requirements.

9.7 The Influence of Price Promotions and Discounts on Consumer Behavior

Businesses can exert much influence on consumer behaviors by utilizing price promotions and discounts, two aspects of pricing strategies that can significantly motivate consumers to make purchasing decisions. This section of the book explains how these two pricing strategies can be implemented and subsequently optimized.

1. **Perceived value:** Consumers often appreciate being given the chance to have access to a product/service through price promotions and discounts. Knowing fully that the product/service is of high quality, their desire for the product/service increases once they are discounted, even if the savings on

price are actually minimal. To reciprocate for this kind of act exhibited by the business hosting the price promotions, consumers will rush such a product, and it may be out of stock within a short period of time.

2. **Purchase intentions:** Pricing strategies such as price promotions, flash sales, discounts, limited-time offers, and promotional events can create a sense of urgency or stimulate purchase intention in consumers. For the fear of missing out, consumers can quickly make purchasing decisions and lock in those discounts on time.

3. **Brand loyalty:** One effective way brands can foster robust, long-lasting relationships with their existing customers is to compensate them through periodic offerings of discounts and price promotions. Consumers normally turn themselves into loyal supporters of brands that duly show them appreciation.

4. **Psychological effects:** The pricing strategies of offering discounts and price promotions somehow produce psychological impacts on consumers. Loss aversion tendency often prompts consumers to act swiftly in taking advantage of the reduction in a product's price to avoid regretting later for failing to jump at the opportunity at the right time.

5. **Competitive advantage:** Businesses can strategically increase their market share by offering discounts and price promotions to win over price-conscious consumers or attract customers from their potential competitors while using the same pricing strategies to prevent their existing customers from switching to other brands. In a very competitive and crowded marketplace, these pricing strategies can create a competitive advantage for any brand adopting them.

6. **Purchase timing:** Offering seasonal sales and holiday promotions can help businesses increase their sales and

maximize revenues and profitability. This is because consumers are usually excited about shopping during these particular periods of the year, buying precious gifts for their loved ones, and being part of some leisure activities.

7. **Perception of quality:** While it is helpful to offer discounts and price promotions to drive sales, brands should endeavor to strike a balance in the course of applying these pricing approaches. Concurrently offering discounts to consumers may cause them to assume that the product is specifically of low quality or the brands doing such price promotions are simply desperate to make some sales.

8. **Price sensitivity:** Consumers respond differently to various discounts and price promotions. Businesses can test different discount offerings to be able to precisely detect consumers' price sensitivity and use that insight to adjust their prices accordingly in order to achieve optimal customer satisfaction.

In summary, it is true that by offering discounts and price promotions, businesses can increase sales and revenues and maximize profitability by influencing consumer behaviors, brand loyalty, perceptions of value, purchasing intentions, and competitive positioning.

Quiz

1. **How do cognitive biases like anchoring bias influence consumer price judgments?**

   a. They encourage impulsive purchasing decisions.

   b. They establish a reference point for evaluating subsequent prices.

   c. They prioritize brand reputation over product quality.

   d. They increase price sensitivity for luxury goods only.

2. **Consumers often use price as a cue for what aspect of a product?**

   a. Brand recognition and popularity.

   b. Product quality

   c. Availability in different retail channels.

   d. The ease of product return and warranty policies.

3. **Which pricing strategy emphasizes the unique benefits a product offers to justify its price?**

   a. Cost-plus pricing

   b. Value-based pricing

   c. Price skimming.

   d. Penetration pricing

4. **How can businesses leverage personalized pricing strategies?**

   a. By offering the same price to all customers regardless of purchase history.

   b. By tailoring prices based on individual customer behavior and preferences.

   c. By focusing solely on maximizing short-term sales.

   d. By minimizing communication about pricing strategies.

5. **What is a key benefit of using value-based pricing?**

   a. It simplifies production cost calculations.

   b. It strengthens the connection between price and perceived customer benefits.

   c. It guarantees the lowest possible price point in the market.

   d. It eliminates the need for market research and competitor analysis.

6. **What pricing psychology tactic involves offering limited-time discounts or promotions?**

   a. Everyday low pricing (EDLP)

   b. Cost leadership pricing

   c. Price ending

   d. Prestige pricing

7. **Price elasticity measures the responsiveness of what changes in price?**

   a. Brand awareness and marketing efforts.

   b. Consumer demand for a product.

   c. Production costs of a product.

   d. The availability of substitute products

8. **Why is flexibility crucial when setting pricing strategies?**

    a. To comply with complex legal requirements.

    b. To adapt to changing consumer preferences and market conditions.

    c. To maintain consistent pricing across all distribution channels.

    d. To minimize the need for market research and competitor analysis.

9. **Beyond just the price tag, what does value-based pricing emphasize?**

    a. Short-term sales volume.

    b. Unique benefits and customer perception of worth.

    c. Production cost efficiency.

    d. Competitive price matching.

10. **Charm pricing, transparent communication, and personalized pricing tactics are all examples of what in pricing psychology?**

    a. Techniques to increase production efficiency.

    b. Strategies to reduce marketing costs.

    c. Methods to optimize consumer perception of price.

    d. Approaches to streamline product development.

Answers	1 – b	2 – b	3 – b	4 – b	5 – b
	6 – c	7 – b	8 – b	9 – b	10 – c

Chapter Summary

- How consumers perceive the price of a product is influenced by their emotions and cognitive biases such as framing and anchoring, not necessarily by logic or simple reasoning.

- The price tag is immaterial; what usually captures consumers' attention is the apparent benefits and value they can derive from using a product/service.

- Endeavor to incorporate psychological pricing tactics in your pricing strategies, such as charm pricing (offering $0.99 instead of $1), personalized pricing that emotionally resonates with consumers, and being transparent while communicating added values to them.

- Naturally, most consumers associate price with a product's quality, indicating that prestigious brands that charge high prices for their premium products are socially justified.

- Businesses need to understand that the demand for their products can be directly affected by sudden changes in price (price elasticity); therefore, they are required to refine their pricing strategies to accommodate this reality.

- It is advisable for businesses to look beyond rationality when deciding a product's price. Sometimes, consumers base their price judgment on biases such as loss aversion (unwilling to miss an opportunity to save on a product's price, even though the savings aren't that much) and image pricing (associating a product's price with its brand image).

- By employing flexible pricing models, utilizing data analytics, and focusing on market segments, a business can come up with an optimal pricing strategy that takes consumers' changing behaviors and market trends into consideration.

Chapter **10**

"P" Number 3: Place or Channels - A Customer Behavior Perspective

The third "P" refers to the distribution channels through which a product or service is distributed. Chapter ten studies the intricate relationship between distribution channels, retail environments, and consumer psychology, uncovering the underlying factors that influence how customers engage with different purchasing channels and shopping experiences. We will investigate how different placed-specific strategies impact customer satisfaction, drive sales, and foster long-term brand loyalty. This will require looking into the comparative significance of outlets versus premium stores, internet and digital channels, and shopping experience designs. It is a fact that businesses need to get their place-related tactics right so as to become leaders in their respective industries.

Key learning objectives should include the reader's understanding of the following:

- Buying satisfaction and consumer behavior

- Outlets, specialty, and premium stores
- Shopping experience designs
- Internet and the Channels Revolution

10.1 Buying Satisfaction and Consumer Behavior

Consumer behaviors are, to a large degree, influenced by some psychological factors influencing their buying satisfaction and shopping experience. Businesses need to understand these motivating factors that are responsible for consumers' purchasing decisions and implement strategies that will increase customer satisfaction and maximize profitability.

10.1.1 Common factors that affect buyer satisfaction

To fully grasp the concept of consumers' buying satisfaction and how it can be enhanced, businesses need to observe, in diverse retail environments, how consumers interact with the products on display, store layouts, and signage. These observations can produce invaluable insights that can be incorporated into decision-making.

1. **Store layout and design:**
   It has been discovered that store layouts and designs realistically influence consumers' purchasing decisions. Some factors like product placement, signage, product descriptions, and aisle width within a store streamline consumers' shopping experience and bring about perceptible customer satisfaction. Therefore, retailers need to focus on how to improve their store layouts in order to encourage continued patronage and subsequently increase sales.

2. **Product placement strategies:**
   The primary goal of all retailers is to place products in strategic locations in their stores to catch the attention of

shoppers hurriedly scanning different shelves. Some of the product placement strategies retailers can employ include but are not limited to eye-level shelving, end-of-aisle displays, and putting related products in adjacent positions one to another. This approach doesn't only enhance the shopping experience but it equally leads to buying satisfaction.

3. **Psychological factors in shopping:**
   It is a fact that consumers' buying satisfaction is directly linked to their psychology, and factors like emotional triggers, biases, and sensory perceptions largely influence their purchasing decisions. Retailers can use their knowledge of this psychological information to proactively engage with their customers and enhance their shopping experiences.

Some examples of the above-mentioned factors are the following:

1. **Supermarket layout optimization:**
   A supermarket chain hired researchers to observe customer behavior within their stores. From a series of observations, they realized that consumers mostly spend a large percentage of their shopping time in aisles that have wider walkways and noticeable product displays. Utilizing the insights from this research, the supermarket decided to remodel its layout, making its aisles wider and conspicuously displaying its products on strategically placed shelves to increase its visibility. This singular effort dramatically increased customer traffic flow inside the supermarket, streamlined navigation and shopping experience, improved consumer satisfaction, and increased sales.

   Macy's, a well-known department store for fashion and clothing accessories, was able to actively engage consumers, achieve higher conversion rates, and grow its sales volume by utilizing the insights obtained from its observational research.[10] Macy's learned that consumers are more likely to purchase a product they can easily see and reach. This realization caused the department store to reorganize its merchandise in a way that products displayed in high-traffic areas are at consumers' eye level and within their reach.

2. **Shopping mall navigation study:**
   To fully understand how streamlined navigation within a shopping mall can reduce congestion, facilitate wayfinding, and improve the shopping experience, Simon Property Group authorized a shopping mall navigation study for all the stores and malls in its portfolio.[11] They discovered, through video surveillance, strategic areas within the malls that are usually congested. The Group responded by redesigning its malls' layouts, signage, and locations of amenities such as toilets and seating arenas to drastically reduce congestion and improve shopping convenience for its customers. This effort has brought about more traffic and encouraged consumers to stay longer while shopping at the malls.

3. **Clothing store fitting room experience**
   Through observational research organized by Zara, customers' fitting room experience was investigated by the company. The retailer has recently unveiled new plans to revolutionize the experience by allowing customers to make reservations on the use of fitting rooms, since this was perceived as a major retail-related problem.[12] New fitting rooms will soon be equipped with e-mirrors for customers

---

10 Rijmenam, Dr Mark van. "Macy's Is Changing The Shopping Experience With Big Data Analytics." Datafloq, March 14, 2014. https://datafloq.com/read/macys-changing-shopping-experience-big-data-analyt/.

11 Group, SVN Commercial Advisory. "How Malls Track Shoppers Inside and Outside Its Doors." *SVN Commercial Advisory Group Commercial Real Estate Services* (blog), June 25, 2019. https://suncoastsvn.com/how-malls-track-consumers/.

12 "ZARA PRESENTS ITS MOST ADVANCED STORE CONCEPT IN MADRID." *Zara.Com.* Accessed November 7, 2024. https://www.zara.com/integration/pressapi/multimedia/64/8d/a29d6e9c4acaaf6c648b842c7f20_original.pdf.

to try new colors and styles without having to try actual clothes.

4. **Fast-food restaurant queue management**
MacDonald's primarily conducted observational research to address the issue of queues at its restaurants, and to specifically ameliorate customers' frustration about this. The company discovered that the long queues were due to inefficient waiting-line management. To increase its customers' satisfaction, MacDonald's implemented some strategies like increasing the number of staff per restaurant to manage queues, adding self-order kiosks, and remodeling the queue layouts to facilitate customers' movement at its restaurants. The efforts help the company to systematically reduce waiting times, increase customer satisfaction scores, and make it possible for customers to accurately order whatever food items they are interested in.

5. **Digital transformation in retail**
Without a doubt, the recent technological advancements in e-commerce and online shopping have revolutionized consumers' shopping experience, challenging traditional retailing in a significant way. It is imperative that any retailer that wants to stay relevant in the industry must operate an online store in addition to their physical stores as more and more shoppers are finding online channels and marketplaces convenient and satisfying for shopping.

6. **Changing consumer preferences**
Modern consumers are interestingly sophisticated, with dynamic preferences that change from time to time. They now prioritize value, quality, convenience, personalization, and exciting shopping experience over every other factor while shopping. To remain relevant among modern-day consumers, improve buying satisfaction, and enjoy robust long-term relationships with them, retailers need to revise their strategies and offer shoppers personalization

opportunities as well as invite them to take advantage of omnichannel shopping approaches.

10.2 Outlets, Specialty and Premium Stores

The retail industry primarily comprises three segments that serve different types of consumers based on their needs and preferences. They are outlets, specialty stores, and premium stores. Current or aspiring retailers need to be aware of the historical development, current nature, and future trends of these segments of retailing before they can successfully tend to their target markets and achieve significant progress in all areas of their business operations.

10.2.1 Historical context

1. **Outlets:** These kinds of stores have their humble beginning from the 20th century, and they were mainly an avenue for manufacturers to sell, directly to consumers, some products they considered to be in excess or marked for discontinuation.

2. **Premium stores:** These are stores that cater to the needs of rich or wealthy people, most especially, those who have the means and are willing to purchase high-quality, premium, luxury products, and enjoy personalized shopping experiences. Stores like Tiffany's and Bloomingdale are categorized as premium stores, which have evolved over the years from being just luxury boutiques or department stores.

3. **Specialty stores:** They are niche retailing outfits that focus primarily on selling specific products or items sought by consumers who are into a specialized event, activity, or expertise. Most of the products in a specialty store aren't

available at the traditional stores, and they can be curated to serve a particular purpose.

10.2.2 Today's landscape

1. **Outlets:** Modern outlets have gone through different stages of evolution. They are currently considered destination shopping centers that attract a large number of value-minded shoppers seeking affordable deals and discounted sales, even for high-quality products. Most cities in the United States have outlets located nearly half an hour's drive from one another. It is possible to find premium products on sale at these outlets. For instance, a Tommy Hilfiger shirt sold at a premium store will be the same as the one on display in an outlet, but with a discounted price.

2. **Premium stores:** Premium stores' scope has gone beyond just being recognized as luxury or boutique stores; nowadays, they have expanded their services to include offering high-end brands, and lifestyle products, and treating their fashionable customers to great customer service.

3. **Specialty stores:** The increasing demand for products sold at specialty stores has led to the establishment of many such stores catering to the needs of consumers looking for unique product categories like electronics, sports, beauty, outdoor gear, historical artifacts, games, etc. Specialty enthusiasts have, in recent years, spread awareness about the uniqueness of specialty products among their groups, encouraging more members to spend their hard-earned money on purchasing those products. Stores like Banana Republic and Victoria's Secret have facilitated the shopping experience for consumers wanting to lay their hands on special products.

10.2.3 Consumer behavior in these channels

This book is about consumer behavior, and it is important that we look at consumers' perspectives when it comes to the issue of retailing.

1. **Outlets:** Most of the consumers that patronize outlets are price-conscious and they are mostly willing to forgo brand prestige and convenience for cost savings, irrespective of how small that might be. Therefore, outlet shoppers are usually excited about taking advantage of discounts, bargains, and promotional sales. They also exhibit the characteristic of comparing product prices for the purpose of choosing the cheaper ones that offer the best value for their money.

2. **Premium stores:** Consumers buying from premium stores are, by nature, less concerned about the prices of the products they are purchasing. Their considerations are based on the products' brands—they prefer brands that reveal prestige, quality, craftsmanship, exclusivity, status symbol, great design, and brand heritage.

3. **Specialty stores:** Specialty store shoppers are primarily after fulfilling their yearnings for expertise, hobbies, authenticity or uniqueness, and historical connections. They are mostly interested in products that will enhance their knowledge, meet their preferences, and excite their curiosities. Consumers who usually patronize specialty stores desire personalized services, and they will become loyal to stores that assist them with curated, unique products that can fulfill their specific desires.

10.2.4 Factors impacting consumer perceptions and purchasing decisions

1. **Pricing:** The three retail segments operate with different pricing models. Outlets offer discounts and promotional

prices to win the hearts of consumers serious about bargains and cost savings. Premium stores, on the other hand, maintain their premium pricing strategy while delivering high-quality, exclusive, and prestigious products that premium shoppers can pay for without a second thought. However, specialty stores offer prices that are competitive and based on the perceived values that specialty shoppers associate with them.

2. **Branding:** Out of the three retail segments, premium stores spend the most on branding and consumer awareness to highlight their offer of luxury, premium products, prestige customer service, and exclusivity. Outlets focus primarily on reaching out to consumers through the promise of a cost-saving and value-based shopping experience. Specialty stores leverage their expertise and niche positioning to build authority and credibility within their target segments.

3. **Product offerings:** Premium stores curate meticulously curated product selections featuring high-end designer labels and limited-edition collections, while outlets offer a broader assortment of merchandise, including overstock, past-season, and factory seconds. Specialty stores specialize in specific product categories, offering unique and hard-to-find items catering to enthusiasts and hobbyists.

10.2.5 Future trends

1. **Omni-channel Integration:** As consumers' preferences change and more people are shopping across different channels (online and offline), it is obvious that outlets, premium stores, and specialty stores have now embraced the omni-channel approach. This doesn't only streamline shoppers' experiences but it also increases their overall satisfaction.

2. **Personalization:** It is clear from all indications that a significant aspect of future retailing trends will involve a

personalized shopping experience. This means that stores will curate and deliver specific products that consumers desire in the convenience of their homes. Premium stores and specialty stores, in particular, will have to utilize data analytics to specifically understand their customers' shopping behaviors in order to properly serve them.

3. **Sustainability:** Consumers' interest in products that are eco-friendly and sourced in ethical ways is increasing across the globe. This indicates that outlets, premium stores, and specialty stores will be required to implement sustainable policies in every facet of their operations to encourage environmentally conscious consumers to patronize them. By promoting activities that support community development and environmental conservation, retailing outfits can consistently win the loyalty of their eco-friendly customers.

The three main segments of the retailing business have already been defined in this chapter, and their characteristics, pricing strategies, branding efforts, and modes of service have equally been described. Using this information, retailers can understand the dynamic terrain of consumer shopping and devise the most appropriate strategies to satisfy their existing customers, as well as prepare to address the future trends' demands.

10.3 Shopping Experience Designs

The modern retail industry is a very competitive landscape, and any retailer that aspires to attract and retain consumers must be proactive in fully understanding their behaviors and serving them based on their individual preferences. To achieve this, it may be necessary to adopt strategies that will create a comfortable shopping experience for consumers. Some of them are explained below:

1. **Customer-centricity:** This concept of customization or personalization gives consumers the unique opportunity to have input into creating products that specifically meet their individual needs or preferences. Nike's "Nike by You", which was formerly known as "NikeiD", exemplifies how this can be done. The company allows consumers to choose their desirable colors, patterns designs, and materials while deciding to purchase Nike footwear or apparel.

2. **Omni-channel integration:** Stores are adopting omni-channels to increase market coverage and foster consumer satisfaction. It is now possible to order products via retailers' physical stores (offline) as well as through online channels such as their websites, e-commerce sites, official Facebook pages, Instagram accounts, WhatsApp, Facebook messengers, etc.
Starbucks, for example, demonstrates that the omnichannel approach works by connecting its app to its physical stores so that consumers can smoothly make reservations, order coffee and snacks, track their orders, pay online, receive their loyalty points, and enjoy other Starbucks' personalized services online and offline.

3. **Sensory stimulation:** When deciding whether to purchase a product or not, if applicable, consumers may use their five senses of smell, touch, sight, hearing, and taste to judge the perceived value of the products. For instance, Lush Cosmetics, through attractive colors and customizable product displays, makes it possible for its customers to immerse themselves in its products' scents. With this approach, consumers are introduced to an exciting shopping experience that will remain in their memory for a long time.

4. **Personalization:** As shown in different examples in this book, Nike has streamlined the shopping experience for its customers through a number of personalized or customized shopping practices. The same effort is noticeable in

Amazon's relationship with its customers all over the world; by recommending specific products to consumers based on their search/browsing histories and previous purchases, Amazon allows them to personalize their shopping experience in a way that perfectly suits their preferences and the retailer achieve a high rate of conversions.

5. **Interactive elements:** New technologies are being used to wow consumers worldwide and provide a unique customer experience. This is a major marketing trend worldwide. Keep track of it. By utilizing Augmented Reality (AR) technology, Sephora gives its customers the chance to try their preferred products virtually on their smartphones. This interactive shopping experience affords them the unique opportunity to see how the products will look exactly on them when purchased. Through this technique, Sephora is able to increase its customer engagement and satisfaction.

6. **Surprise and delight:** This is not new to marketing at all. Small gifts have been around forever. The point is to question this factor and add it to your marketing experience. Glossier frequently surprises customers with unexpected gifts and free samples included in their orders. These small gestures of appreciation delight customers and exceed their expectations, fostering loyalty and positive word-of-mouth.

7. **Community building:** With the Internet at hand, building a community and strengthening the relationship with your tribe is a must. To foster a sense of community and togetherness around its brand, Lululemon consistently sponsors events such as workshops and runs clubs and yoga classes. The company uses this strategy to create a strong bond among its customers who are fitness enthusiasts. The organized events become an avenue for Lululemon customers to mingle with one another or socialize, network, and share useful experiences with one another.

All the points discussed in this section indicate that for a retailer to differentiate itself from others in the marketplace, it needs to be customer-centric, implement omni channels, stimulate the senses of its existing or targeted customer base, and promote interactive shopping experiences.

10.4 Internet and the Channels Revolution

It is an undeniable fact that the Internet has revolutionized the retail industry as it opens it up to many opportunities for consumers. As part of the benefits, consumers can now engage in web-based shopping through e-commerce sites and other online marketplaces, from the comfort of their homes. Digital retailing has been evolving these past decades, giving consumers more control over their shopping experiences and influencing their behaviors or habits.

This section looks at the comprehensive benefits of internet-based retailing for consumers as well as considering the impacts of this revolution on the retail industry (and retailers) as a whole.

10.4.1 Impact of the Internet on consumer behavior

From the perspective of consumer behavior, the Internet is significantly impacting the ways consumers discover and shop for products and services. Some of the apparent benefits of the Internet revolution in the retail industry are highlighted below:

1. **Convenience and accessibility:** E-commerce and online marketplaces offer unprecedented shopping convenience and accessibility to consumers. All that modern-day shoppers need to do is to have access to the Internet, order products online, and have them delivered to their homes, thereby eliminating the tedious commute to physical stores. Even though slow delivery time is still an issue with e-commerce, businesses like Uber Eats and PedidosYa (popularly referred to as last-mile apps) are working seriously on speedy delivery.

2. **Expanded product selection:** Consumers can now have access to a wide range of products irrespective of their geographical locations. Online marketplaces, like Alibaba, have broken down geographical barriers and allowed shoppers worldwide to order any products of their choice. From niche products to mainstream ones, based on their individual preferences, consumers can order and pay for any products they desire and have them shipped across different continents to their homes, usually within a few weeks. Alibaba, for instance, allows consumers to order directly from local manufacturers based in China.

3. **Personalization and targeting:** The internet has streamlined retailers' intentions to actively engage with their customers on an individualized level. Nowadays, retailers can use their customers' browsing/search histories, demographic information, and unique preferences to retarget them with products/services that perfectly meet their specific needs.

4. **Information and reviews:** Unlike before, the internet aids modern-day consumers in making informed purchasing decisions. With the stockpile of online reviews, user-generated content, and product information available on the internet, consumers can quickly identify which product will better serve the purpose they want it for. The internet can be credited for improving consumer shopping experience and helping retailers broadcast vital information about their brands to people all over the world.

10.4.2 Transformation of e-commerce platforms and online marketplaces:

The internet plays some significant roles in the transformation of e-commerce, and highlighted below are some of the internet-inspired improvements in e-commerce:

1. **Rise of e-commerce giants:** Amazon, Alibaba, and eBay are, undoubtedly, the leading e-commerce platforms, and their

personalized services have dramatically improved consumer shopping experiences and satisfaction. These e-commerce giants make a wide range of products available to consumers and offer them competitive prices. By using algorithms and data analytics, these e-commerce behemoths learn about consumer behaviors and recommend useful, moderately priced products to their loyal customers accordingly.

2. **Social commerce:** With the advent of social media such as Facebook, WhatsApp, Instagram, Pinterest, etc., retailers are utilizing social engagements and content to drive prospective customers to their products/services displayed or advertised on these social media platforms. These platforms' social commerce features make it possible for businesses to sell their products, get paid, and be reviewed. On certain occasions, consumers may be directed to call a particular phone number, login into retailers' e-commerce websites, or be implored to purchase their desirable products at any of the businesses' physical stores. There are billions of daily active users on all these social media platforms combined, and that explains how powerful the evolving social commerce is.

3. **Emergence of online marketplaces:** Small and medium-sized businesses will always be grateful for the invention of the Internet, which has liberalized the retail industry. It is now possible for a small and obscure company to compete on equal footing with a large, well-known brand by selling the same product to a large number of consumers around the globe. Online marketplaces like Amazon, Etsy, Shopify, and Depoop allow small and medium-sized businesses to open their online stores on their platforms for a fee. This rare opportunity to sell to consumers globally has expanded niche marketplaces and eventually led to creative entrepreneurship.

10.4.3 Challenges and opportunities for businesses:

These are some of the issues businesses need to pay serious attention to:

1. **Adapting to digital transformations:** To be competitive, increase market reach, win over new customers, and increase profitability, businesses need to embrace and adapt to digital transformations. This requires that they set up e-commerce websites, spend on digital marketing, and integrate omnichannel capability on their online stores or platforms.

2. **Managing customer expectations:** It is important for businesses to understand that digital consumers also have some expectations that must be met. These include excellent customer service, fast responsiveness, and a streamlined shopping experience. When consumers are satisfied with the quality of products offered and their transparent prices, they will naturally be loyal to the brands taking good care of them. This will eventually lead to repeat patronage, and customers will automatically become brand ambassadors to spread the good news about the great products they had previously utilized.

3. **Navigating competitive dynamics:** Any business that wants to stay relevant and agile in the highly competitive digital retail terrain must undertake the following processes— embrace innovations, be aware of and attend to consumers' evolving preferences, pay attention to the dynamic trends in its industry, offer high-quality products/services to consumers, give memorable brand experience to its customers, and separate itself from the pack through unique value proposition.

It is clear from the facts stated in this section that the Internet can be credited for revolutionizing the retail industry in a good way. However, businesses need to wake up to both the opportunities and challenges the digital retail industry offers.

Quiz

1. **How does consumer behavior impact businesses?**
   a. It has no significant effect.
   b. It shapes buying satisfaction, ultimately influencing business success.
   c. It only affects marketing strategies.
   d. It solely determines product development.

2. **Understanding which factors are crucial for creating positive shopping experiences.**
   a. Legal regulations on product safety.
   b. Psychological factors that influence consumer decisions.
   c. Production costs of the goods.
   d. The physical size of the retail store.

3. **Specialty stores typically differentiate themselves through what factor?**
   a. Offering discounted prices.
   b. Providing expert knowledge and service in a specific product category.
   c. Carrying a wide variety of unrelated products.
   d. Focusing on established brand names.

4. **Which concept emphasizes putting the customer at the center of all business decisions?**
   a. Cost leadership (minimizing production costs).
   b. Customer-centricity (focusing on customer needs and satisfaction).
   c. Price skimming (charging a premium price initially).
   d. Market segmentation (targeting specific customer groups).

5. **What are some advantages of online shopping for consumers?**

    a. Convenience of shopping from anywhere at any time.

    b. Access to a wider selection of products than physical stores.

    c. Potentially lower prices due to reduced overhead costs.

    d. The inability to physically examine products before purchase.

6. **What is a challenge that businesses face in the age of digital transformation?**

    a. The internet eliminates the need for physical stores altogether.

    b. Adapting to changing consumer expectations and online shopping habits.

    c. The complete dominance of large e-commerce companies.

    d. A lack of data on customer preferences and buying behavior.

7. **How can businesses leverage surprise to enhance the customer experience?**

    a. Implementing a complicated loyalty program.

    b. Offering unexpected free gifts or upgrades.

    c. Maintaining consistently high prices.

    d. Limiting customer interaction with store staff.

8. **Observational research helps in analyzing what aspects of a store?**

    a. Financial performance and profitability.

    b. Store layout, product placement, and consumer psychology.

    c. The effectiveness of marketing campaigns.

    d. The quality of customer service interactions.

9. **The chapter states that "consumer behavior is king." What does this imply?**

   a. Consumer preferences are the most important factor for any business.

   b. Businesses should focus solely on understanding consumer psychology.

   c. There is no need for businesses to invest in marketing or advertising.

   d. Consumers are always rational and logical in their decision-making.

10. **Why is understanding "psychological factors" important for creating positive shopping experiences?**

    a. It allows businesses to manipulate consumers into buying more.

    b. It helps businesses predict consumer behavior and cater to their needs.

    c. It eliminates the need for high-quality customer service.

    d. It discourages consumers from browsing or spending time in stores.

Answers	1 – b	2 – b	3 – b	4 – b	5 – a
	6 – b	7 – b	8 – b	9 – a	10 – b

Chapter Summary

◆ Consumer behavior directly impacts buying satisfaction and a business's overall success. Understanding these behaviors is crucial.

◆ Psychological factors significantly influence consumer behavior. Understanding these factors helps create positive shopping experiences.

◆ With observational research methodology, which involves monitoring consumer behaviors, analyzing product placements, and appraising store layouts in physical retailing spaces, retailers can further understand their customer's behaviors and preferences.

◆ Thanks to the digital revolution, consumers can now access a lot of information about their desired products and enjoy convenient, personalized, and satisfying shopping experiences. Retailers can then utilize data analytics to properly understand their customers' behaviors.

◆ Based on diverse consumer preferences, the retailing industry is divided into three unique formats or segments: The outlets are for consumers actively seeking discounts and promotional prices; premium stores are specifically known for their high-quality products, which may be expensive; specialty stores cater to the needs of consumers seeking expertise and special product knowledge.

◆ It is important to always remember that perception is key for the growth of all three retail formats because consumers' purchasing decisions are influenced by the inherent values they perceive in the products on offer, in addition to product prices and branding.

◆ It is generally believed that the future of retail will depend largely on how many of the existing retailing outfits embrace and smoothly integrate omnichannel approaches into their day-to-day operations, as well as personalizing their services to meet consumers' expectations. It is also essential that they focus on sustainability as many consumers nowadays are gravitating towards businesses that are eco-friendly.

◆ Retailers can choose to streamline the shopping experience for consumers by ensuring that they have access to the products they want via both online and offline channels. Moreover, engaging consumers in sensory stimulation can result in better interaction between retailers and their targeted consumer segments.

◆ Offering a personalized shopping experience can cause consumers to become loyal patrons or fans of any brand.

◆ Retailers that include interactive elements in their shopping processes will surely increase their customers' engagement and satisfaction.

◆ Creating a sense of surprise and delight for customers can foster positive brand perception and loyalty.

◆ Fostering a sense of community around your brand can strengthen customer relationships and loyalty.

This page is intentionally left blank

Chapter 11

"P" Number 4: Promotion or Communication - A Customer Behavior Perspective

In Chapter eleven, we will be focusing on consumer-centric marketing communications. Businesses need to understand how to craft messaging that strategically resonates with consumers throughout their shopping experience, from the moment of their initial awareness of a product to repeat purchases. The chapter will explore techniques for assessing consumer product knowledge at each stage of the journey and selecting appropriate media channels to reach and engage target audiences. Furthermore, readers will gain insights into the vital role of creativity in communication campaigns, the distinctions between promotions and strategic advertising, and emerging trends shaping the future of marketing communications.

Key learning objectives should include the reader's understanding of the following:

- Defining marketing communications

- Understanding the consumer journey, consumer decision-making stage
- The role of a creative brief
- Assessing consumer product knowledge and its methods
- Selecting the right media channels
- Integration and creativity in marketing communications
- Promotions vs. strategic advertising and differentiating among tactics
- The role of influencers, brands, and product image
- Measuring the success of a marketing campaign

11.1 Defining Marketing Communications

Marketing communications involves implementing different strategies and techniques necessary for promoting products and services so as to influence consumer behaviors (and, of course, their shopping patterns) and drive sales. This section provides the foundational information for the dynamic concept of marketing communications, highlighting the key principles that can lead to successful marketing communications.

Marketing communications, usually shortened as MarCom, refers to a combination of techniques and processes employed by organizations to pass vital information about their products and services to their target audience. Essentially, MarCom includes processes such as sales promotions, social media marketing, public relations, direct marketing, and other types of communication that can be used to create awareness about a product/service, develop consumers' interests in it, and create long-lasting engagements with customers.

11.1.1 Key concepts related to marketing communications

1. **Objectives and goals:** Businesses invest in marketing communications to achieve certain objectives or goals.

These may include but are not limited to creating awareness for the existing and new products and their great features, expanding into a new marketplace to drive sales, or influencing consumers' perceptions and turning them into loyal customers. It is advisable for businesses to have specific objectives when engaging in marketing communications. They will be able to focus their efforts solely on consumer segments where they can accomplish tangible results, crafting effective messaging that will resonate with them.

2. **Audience analysis:** Analyzing which market segments to target with specific messaging is, perhaps, the first step in the process of undertaking effective marketing communications. A well-coordinated audience analysis should reveal the dominant demographics, consumer behaviors, preferences, and psychographics so that businesses can convey the right messaging to them in a convincing and proper manner.

3. **Integrated marketing communications (IMC):** Integrated marketing communications (IMCs) allow businesses to deliver consistent and harmonized marketing messaging across different communication channels and media. This indicates that businesses can take advantage of diverse approaches to marketing communications, which may include but are not limited to public relations, digital marketing, advertising, and other communication outlets. Consumers will have the benefit of receiving unified messaging from the same company irrespective of the channel or medium employed.

4. **The communication process:** It is important for marketers to have a deep understanding of the communication process which, in practice, involves encoding messages, choosing the most suitable communication channels, and conveying the messages to the targeted audience so that they can properly decode the messages and produce appropriate responses. In essence, businesses should draft the most

impactful messages and transmit them to consumers
through their preferred communication channels to be able
to elicit sensible responses from them.

5. **The role of creative briefs:** The primary purpose of creative
briefs is to act as a roadmap for businesses while creating
their marketing campaigns. A typical creative brief will
highlight the main objectives of the marketing campaign,
its target audience, success metrics, messaging strategies,
and creative concepts. When several teams are involved in
the creation of a marketing campaign, creative briefs are
useful for spelling out the parts to be played by each team
so as to ensure cohesion and effectiveness of the marketing
messaging.

11.2 Understanding the Consumer Journey

A consumer's journey with a business is not usually a straight
line but a cyclical one that is largely influenced by various factors.
These factors may include the kind of product, consumers'
personal preferences, and other external influences. Therefore,
consumers make their decisions about a particular product in
stages, and it is helpful for businesses that want to retain their
existing customers or capture new ones to understand these stages
so as to create meaningful and impactful marketing messaging
that can move consumers to make favorable purchasing decisions.

11.2.1 Exploring the consumer decision-making process

1. **Awareness stage**
This is the first stage in a consumer's journey, and it is the
period that a consumer expresses desire or interest in a
product/service because of its perceived value or usefulness.
There are some factors that come into play during the
awareness stage. They include the degree of familiarity
with the brand, the level of engagement/involvement with

the product/service, and the frequency of purchase. For low-involvement product categories such as groceries, consumers may discover that they need the product while shopping at a greengrocer's. On the other hand, for high-involvement products like luxury goods, consumers' desire may be triggered by a piece of advertising or social pressure.

It is important to note that high-involvement/low-involvement (HI-LI) does not depend on categories though it helps in the teaching process and most books express it so. It is based on each target characteristic. Some people buy a cereal bar that is closer to their hand in the supermarket aisle, while some people choose the right bar given that they are foodies or vegans, or they are going to use it for a sports practice. These facts turn them into a high involvement (HI) target market. Alternatively, when you are buying an apartment, you will always be a HI target market given the expenditure size, and high exit costs, among other factors.

2. **Consideration stage**

Once consumers are aware of their needs, they enter the consideration stage, where they evaluate available options and alternatives. This stage can vary significantly across categories based on factors such as product complexity, perceived risk, and the presence of competing brands. In categories like electronics or automobiles, consumers may conduct extensive research (they are HI), compare features, read reviews, and seek recommendations before making a decision. In contrast, for impulse-driven categories like snacks or beverages (LI categories), consideration may be brief, with consumers relying on habit, price promotions, or brand loyalty. There are categories where consumers do have high loyalty levels, like Nescafe for instant coffee and Colgate for toothpaste, which generally make them an LI case.

3. **Evaluation and purchase stage**

   At this stage, consumers are cutting down the options/
   alternatives they can choose from and focusing on the
   particular product they believe will be the most useful for
   them. They will make their purchasing decisions based
   on the product's price, brand recognition, quality, and
   perceived value. How long and intense this stage can
   be dependent on the consumers' level of involvement,
   perceived risks linked to the purchase, and how much
   admiration consumers have for the brand.

   For utilitarian products like household goods or
   personal care items, consumers may prioritize practical
   considerations such as price and convenience. In contrast,
   for products with strong emotional appeal like fashion
   or beauty products, the evaluation stage may involve
   subjective criteria such as style, aesthetics, and brand image.
   There are important debates in categories like cars, where
   practical considerations seem to be predominant in the
   market.

4. **Post-purchase evaluation and loyalty**

   Consumers engage in post-purchase evaluation to ascertain
   the usefulness of the product they have spent their hard-
   earned money on. This also happens to be an important
   stage for businesses because consumers, based on the
   satisfaction derived from using the product, may choose
   to become loyal advocates for the brand and engage in
   repeat purchases. It is advisable that businesses pay serious
   attention to customer feedback and post-sales services that
   can considerably improve consumer experiences, most
   especially for products/services in the hospitality and
   technology categories. On the other hand, for one-time
   purchases, businesses can concentrate on creating long-
   lasting, remarkable experiences for consumers. Lexus,
   for instance, keeps close contact with their customers,
   reminding them directly about the time for an after-sales

service. Their product experience is greatly enhanced by the after-sales service, looking for a repeat purchase pattern.

11.3 The Customer Lifetime Value Model

The last comment, allows us to elaborate on the customer-lifetime value or CLV model. Businesses utilize the concept of CLV to project the possible amount of revenue they can be able to generate from every customer throughout their transactional relationships. CLV, as a business tool, gives businesses a sneak peek into a possible net profit derivable from transacting with a consumer over a lifetime.

Here's how a typical CLV model works:

1. **Revenue projection:** The CLV model can be used to compute how much a customer will spend on a product within a specified period, say 5 to 10 years (if the customer stays with the brand). The CLV estimation takes into account factors such as average transaction value, how often the customer makes purchases, and extra revenue streams from subscription fees and other additional service charges.

2. **Cost allocation:** Once the total revenue derivable from a customer has been successfully estimated, businesses also need to calculate the costs required to serve the customer. The costs may include expenses on sales, marketing communication, customer service, and other indirect expenses linked to serving the customer.

3. **Discounting future cash flows:** Since the inflation rate in the future cannot be precisely predicted, it is usually assumed that a dollar now may be worth less in the near future. Hence, businesses have a way of protecting their future cash flows, which involves applying a specific discounting rate to their current cash flow value based on historical inflation rates.

4. **Customer churn rate:** It is a fact that not all customers will stay with a brand forever; some of them will leave or switch to other brands. Hence, to ensure that their CLV estimations are realistic, most businesses apply a churn or attrition rate to their CLV modeling. This is the rate that calculates the possible number of customers that may, for one reason or the other, stop buying products from businesses in the future.

5. **Strategic decision-making:** Having a deep understanding of the implications of CLV, businesses can make strategic decisions that will improve the customer experience so as to reduce churn rate and help them maintain considerable cash flows for a long time. Therefore, it would be necessary for businesses to engage in pricing optimization, resource allocation, customer acquisition strategies, and customer retention processes.

Understanding consumer journey stages and the usefulness of the CLV model can help businesses improve their communication processes and reap huge benefits from undertaking strategies that will drastically reduce their churn rates.

11.4 Methods for Assessing Consumer Product Knowledge

A whole section on marketing research has been developed in this book in Chapter 6. A summary of the appropriate techniques for assessing consumer product knowledge is presented in this section. Marketers need to be fully aware of how much understanding consumers have about their products/services—this will show how effective their marketing strategies have been, and how consumers are actively engaging with the products/services they have promoted. Here are several methods commonly used for assessing consumer product knowledge:

With surveys and questionnaires, we can have tools to understand which part of the consumer journey the target market is. Surveys are critical in order to understand and measure where these people are. Through focus group interactions, marketers can qualitatively probe consumers about their product knowledge by asking them open-ended questions and engaging them in rapt discussions. It is possible to unearth a lot of information about consumers' beliefs, experiences, and perceptions concerning a product through this approach. More importantly, focus groups allow marketers to explore deeper into consumers' unexpressed nuances and misconceptions in order to discover their pressing needs.

With in-depth interviews and one-on-one discussions, marketers can unravel a great deal of information about consumers' knowledge levels in relation to a particular product. From consumers' thoughtful responses, marketers can understand consumers' motivations, decision-making methods, and purchasing attitudes. In-depth interviews can further help marketers discover consumers' actual motives and their individual perspectives that may influence their knowledge of a product's attributes.

Marketers can use observational research to tremendously learn about consumers' preferences, product knowledge levels, and behaviors. This observation research is predominantly conducted inside a brand's natural setting like its store or shopfront. Mystery shoppers or preselected shoppers are contracted to observe how other consumers interact with the products on display on the shelves in the stores, and what motivates them to make their purchasing decisions.

Using digital platforms such as e-commerce websites, marketers can understand consumers' preferences, track their online behaviors, and discover the gaps in their product knowledge. When consumers go online to shop, their search keywords or search queries can show a lot of information about what they are seeking online. Analyzing e-commerce websites' traffic and user engagement metrics can reveal how consumers engage with product pages, check out the product descriptions, and explore information online.

The two main advantages of conducting a brand awareness study are that it allows marketers to know how effective or penetrating their marketing effort has been, and how influential it is in contributing to consumers' product knowledge. Marketers usually carry out brand awareness studies to see if consumers have familiarized themselves with a brand and can easily distinguish it from the other brands on the shelves. One of the tools marketers often use to measure consumers' brand awareness levels is a survey, it can track brand recall, brand association, and brand recognition.

By offering free trials and time-limited demonstrations of a product, marketers can obtain some insights from the practice as consumers' reactions, usage behavior, and feedback can say a lot about how they like the product, or how much product knowledge they have acquired. This is a unique opportunity for marketers to learn about the consumers' perceptions of the product firsthand.

By combining the methods described above, marketers can easily identify consumers' preferences, behavioral patterns, perceptions, and product knowledge levels. With these insights, marketers can better tailor their marketing efforts, communication strategies, and product offerings in a way that meets consumers' needs/preferences and increases their loyal engagement with the product.

11.5 Selecting the Right Media Channels

The very first step in achieving success in marketing is selecting the right media channels. It is no coincidence that a large part of the marketing budget is spent on marketing channels so that marketers can utilize the most effective medium to reach their targeted audience. Table 11.1 provides an elaboration on various media channels available for advertising and promotion.

| Table 11.1 | Various media channels |

Medium	Description	Advantages	Disadvantages
Television (Open TV)	A powerful medium for mass advertising, ideal for businesses with large budgets.	• Mass exposure • Wide audience demographic • Creative flexibility with audiovisual content	• High production costs • Ongoing competition for viewership • Limited targeting compared to digital ads
Radio	Audio messages delivered via FM, AM, and online stations, reaching audiences on the go.	• Flexible ad format • Cost-effective • Good for local targeting	• Limited visual impact • Fragmented audience • Declining listenership
Print Media	Newspapers and magazines provide a more intimate ad experience through physical formats.	• Target audience segmentation • Physically accessible • Long shelf life	• Declining readership • Limited reach compared to digital • Longer lead times for ad placement
Outdoor Advertising	Billboards and posters that are highly visible in public spaces.	• Prominently visible • Repeated exposure for reinforcement	• Limited message retention • Effectiveness depends on location • Susceptible to weather conditions

Medium	Description	Advantages	Disadvantages
Search Engine Advertising	Targets users actively seeking specific keywords or phrases.	• Precise targeting • Cost-effective with PPC model	• Competitive and expensive for popular keywords • Requires ongoing optimization
Display Advertising	Visual ads in various formats on websites and apps.	• Wide audience reach • Visually appealing • Various formats available	• Can be intrusive • Ad blockers may reduce visibility
Social Media Advertising	Targets consumers based on behavior and interests, facilitating user interaction.	• Streamlined targeting • Encourages audience engagement • Provides analytic insights	• Difficult to achieve long-term organic reach • Time-consuming to manage • Users may experience ad fatigue
Video Advertising	Engaging visuals and storytelling to convey messages across devices.	• Captivates attention • Effective for complex messages • Broad reach across devices	• High production costs • Skippable ads may limit reach • Requires compelling content

Medium	Description	Advantages	Disadvantages
Native Advertising	Blends with the surrounding content, appearing as articles or social media posts.	• Not disruptive • Increases brand trust • Can be contextually targeted	• Requires disclosures to avoid misleading users • Effectiveness depends on audience engagement • May confuse readers
Email Marketing	Direct communication with subscribers through personalized messages.	• Direct communication • Useful for engaging active leads • Customizable content	• Variable open and click-through rates • May be considered spam • Requires list management
Content Marketing	Curates relevant content to engage and educate the target audience over time.	• Attracts organic traffic via SEO • Establishes thought leadership • Educates readers	• Takes time to see results • Requires continuous promotion and optimization • Time-consuming to create high-quality content
Affiliate Marketing	Performance-based model where promoters earn commissions for sales.	• No upfront costs • Can drive significant sales through partnerships	• Requires monitoring of affiliate relationships • Susceptible to fraud • Commission fees can cut profits

Medium	Description	Advantages	Disadvantages
Influencer Marketing	Leverages social media personalities to promote products to dedicated audiences.	• Relies on influencer credibility • Effective in niche markets • Authentic recommendations resonate well	• Difficult to measure ROI • Time-consuming to find credible influencers • Authenticity issues can affect marketing effectiveness
Podcast Advertising	Sponsors insert messages into podcast episodes targeting engaged listeners.	• Emphasizes brand storytelling • Reaches well-defined audience • Depends on niche relevance	• Smaller audience reach compared to other channels • Limited targeting opportunities • Must align with audience preferences
Mobile Advertising	Ads delivered on smartphones and tablets, allowing for geo-targeting.	• Geo-targeting capabilities • Interactive ad formats • Integrates well with digital channels	• Privacy concerns • Ad blocking by service providers • Small screen sizes can hinder visibility
Programmatic Advertising	Automated buying and selling of ads across channels.	• Scalable and efficient • Access to large inventory • Real-time optimization and targeting	• Potential for fraud • Complex platforms • Brand safety concerns

Medium	Description	Advantages	Disadvantages
Retargeting/ Remarketing	Shows ads to past visitors to renew interest in a brand.	• Reconnects with previous users • Encourages personalized advertising • Reinforces brand messaging	• Can annoy users if overdone • Frequency control needed • Must target appropriate segments

Additional marketing channels that are worth mentioning in this section are provided in Table 11.2. Each of these platforms offers unique opportunities and challenges for advertisers, depending on their target audience, industry, and marketing objectives. Understanding the nuances of each platform is essential for creating effective advertising strategies and maximizing ROI.

These are general pros and cons associated with each internet advertising medium, and the effectiveness of each method can vary depending on factors such as industry, target audience, campaign objectives, and budget.

Table 11.2   Additional marketing channels

Platform	Description	Pros	Cons
YouTube	The world's largest video-sharing platform for uploading, viewing, and sharing videos.	• Extensive reach (2 billion active users) • Diverse ad formats (non-skippable, skippable, etc.) • Targeting options based on interests and behaviors • Analytics available	• High competition • High production costs • Ineffectiveness of skippable ads if not viewed

Platform	Description	Pros	Cons
Instagram	A photo and video-sharing application owned by Facebook.	• Visual focus for product display • Large user base (1 billion active users) • Various ad formats • Advanced targeting options	• Limited link placement • Increasing competition • High-quality content needed to stand out
Facebook	The largest social network platform with billions of active users.	• Massive user base (2.8 billion monthly users) • Multiple ad formats • Extensive targeting options • Useful analytics via Ads Manager	• Declining organic reach • Ad fatigue among users • Rising competition leading to increased costs
TikTok	An app for sharing short-form videos that can go viral.	• Rapid growth (11 billion users) • Engaging short-form content • High viral potential • Diverse ad formats	• Limited targeting compared to other platforms • Brand safety concerns • Predominantly young audience

Platform	Description	Pros	Cons
Google Ads	An online advertising platform for placing ads on Google search results, YouTube, and partner websites.	• Extensive reach across various platforms • Multiple targeting options • Diverse ad formats • Useful analytics tools	• High competition for keywords • Requires ongoing optimization • Limited control over ad placement
Twitter (X)	A microblogging platform for sharing real-time experiences and news.	• Real-time engagement • Wide reach (330 million monthly users) • Various ad formats • Targeting options based on behaviors and interests	• Character limit enforces conciseness • Content saturation may affect visibility • Engagement challenges with competing content
LinkedIn	A professional networking platform for career-oriented individuals.	• Professional audience (740 million members) • Various ad formats • Targeting based on industry and job title • Useful for B2B marketing	• Higher advertising costs • Limited organic reach • Primarily focused on B2B marketing

Platform	Description	Pros	Cons
Snapchat	A messaging app known for disappearing content and augmented reality features.	• Young audience (500 million active users) • Immersive multimedia content • Various ad formats	• Limited targeting options • Disappearing content limits longevity • Frequent platform updates require user adaptation
Pinterest	A visual discovery platform for saving and sharing ideas.	• Visual discovery for personal projects • High purchase intent • Various ad formats • Targeting based on interests and shopping behaviors	• Niche audience (primarily women) • Requires consistent fresh content • Competition increases ad placement costs
Netflix	A subscription-based streaming service with a wide audience reach.	• Large subscriber base for wide audience reach • Original content provides sponsorship opportunities	• Limited advertising options • Ad-free experience limits traditional ad placement
Amazon Prime Video	A streaming service with a diverse content library and original programming.	• Diverse content appeals to various audiences • Opportunities for product integration and sponsorship	• Limited ad inventory • Competitive landscape limits visibility

Platform	Description	Pros	Cons
Disney+	A subscription service known for family-friendly content.	• Positive brand association • Family-friendly content appeals to parents and children	• Ad-free model limits advertising opportunities • Limited targeting options
Spotify	One of the largest podcast platforms offering a range of content across demographics.	• Broad reach across demographics • Targeted advertising based on listener behaviors	• Ad skipping options reduce effectiveness • Ad clutter may diminish impact
Apple Podcasts	A widely available podcast platform integrated into Apple devices.	• Native integration on Apple devices • Leverages Apple's credibility for brand trust	• Limited ad targeting options • Fragmented ecosystem complicates audience reach
Google Podcasts	A podcast platform benefiting from Google's search capabilities.	• Discoverability through search • Cross-platform compatibility	• Limited monetization options • Data privacy concerns may affect advertisers' credibility

11.6 Insights Into Integration and Creativity in Marketing Communications

Integration and creativity play an important role in marketing communications, because they encourage engagement, expand brand awareness, and motivate consumer actions. Highlighted below are ways integration and creativity can revolutionize a brand's marketing efforts.

By implementing integrated marketing communications (IMC) brands can convey harmonized and consistent messaging to their target audience. A successful IMC strategy employs a combination of channels to reach out to consumers, through digital marketing, public relations, advertising, social media, direct marketing, and others. When consumers receive consistent and coherent messages from a brand, they consider such a brand to be credible, and this positive perception can influence their levels of interaction and engagement with it.

It is estimated that consumers in the United States are exposed to about 4000 to 10,000 brand messages every day. For a brand to stand out from all the noise out there, it has to be creative in delivering its communication to consumers. The overwhelming brand messages consumers daily get from social media posts, television ads, emails, mobile apps, billboards, radio ads, product packaging, etc. compels them to be very selective. Nowadays, it takes creativity and innovation in communication to be able to catch consumers' divided attention. Therefore, to outsmart other competitors, a brand needs to do three essential things. One, it must have a compelling and clear brand message; two, be innovative and creative in delivering it; and three, the cogent message must be repeated until it resonates with consumers.

When brand messages are communicated creatively and appropriately to consumers, using the available technologies, it can invoke genuine emotions in consumers' minds and cause them to feel strongly connected to the brand, becoming its loyal ambassadors. Creativity in communication can be in the form of using attractive visuals in designing brand messages, adopting the latest technologies to deliver the messages to consumers, and interacting with them to understand the impact of the communication on them.

The essence of integrated marketing communications is to make sure that consumers are exposed to the same brand messages across all channels. This consistency won't only be instrumental in reinforcing brand reputation and brand identity, but it will also cause consumers to trust the brand and connect with it emotionally. The stronger the emotional connection consumers have to a brand, the more robust the brand affinity. Every brand hopes to have loyal customers around them; this is why it is important that they come up with innovative and creative methods for maintaining great relationships with consumers. Some of the approaches adopted by brands to achieve this include using emotional storytelling, interactive campaigns, gamified experiences, and experiential marketing.

In summary, it is apparent that integration and creativity are vital parts of successful marketing communication, making it possible for brands to deliver harmonized and coherent messages across all channels. By adopting an integrated approach, brands can foster a genuine connection with consumers and enjoy long-time patronage from them.

11.7 Promotions vs. Strategic Advertising - Differentiating Among Tactics

One important discussion that is often made at most businesses' marketing departments is whether to employ strategic advertising or promotions. While the two processes appear similar, they indeed serve different purposes and utilize different tactics. However, there are some factors that should be put into consideration before undertaking strategic advertising or promotions. First, what is the current consumer journey? Second, will a promotion encourage the consumer to purchase a product on offer? Third, how to build profitability in the promotional effort?

Let's look at the key features of promotions and strategic advertising.

11.7.1 Promotions

1. **Short-term focus:** Promotions are usually used on a short-term basis to achieve a specific goal, whether to get new customers, sell out excess inventory, or fulfill seasonal demand.

2. **Incentives and discounts:** Consumers are usually motivated by promotions to make a purchase or subscribe to a service due to some incentives such as discounts, rebates, time-limited offers, coupons, loyalty programs, cashbacks, or contests.

3. **Direct response:** Promotions are usually designed to get consumers to produce a direct response, which may be buying a product or signing up for a service.

4. **Tactical flexibility:** Promotions are flexible, and they can be refined to accommodate changes in market situations, pricing, sales volumes, and competitors' influences.

11.7.2 Strategic advertising

1. **Long-term brand building:** The primary objective of strategic advertising is to build awareness around a brand and influence consumers' perceptions of the brand, leading to a mutually beneficial relationship between the brand and consumers. It also helps reinforce brand identity and position in the marketplace.

2. **Emotional appeal:** Strategic advertising makes use of compelling storytelling and motivational messages to emotionally connect with consumers. It is possible for a strong bond and enduring relationships to exist between brands and consumers if the brand messages resonate strongly with them.

3. **Broad reach and frequency:** Strategic advertising utilizes mass media to reach a large population of consumers via channels such as digital platforms, radio, television, and print to deliver consistent and unified messaging to them, emphasizing brand identity and credibility.

4. **Brand integration:** Strategic advertising involves incorporating a multi-channel approach, ensuring that the same, unified messaging is broadcast to consumers across all media. This is capable of bolstering brand values, positioning, and attributes.

In summary, both promotions and strategic advertising are required for business success but, as shown above, they are implemented for different purposes. While promotions incentivize consumers short term to make a purchase or take a definite action, strategic advertising is a long-term play, and it is primarily useful for creating brand awareness, increasing brand equity, and for fostering long-term relationships with consumers.

11.8 The Role of Influencers, Brands, and Product Image

The digital-age business terrain has rapidly been changing because of the impact of influencers. Influencers are those who, on digital platforms, create a dedicated followership through credibility, authority in some ideas or expertise, and trust. Businesses are now working with influencers to promote their brand awareness, and products/services, and hope to sell to those influencers' followers who consume content and pieces of advice dished out by the influencers. Through product mentions and recommendations, influencers can help a business expand its market reach and multiply sales. This section of the book looks into the interrelation between influencers, brands, and product image. The following points discuss how influencers can help a brand:

1. **Building brand awareness:** Influencers are currently assisting brands to enjoy more visibility, and recognition, and score better patronage. Through engaging content, influencers can introduce brands and/or their products to their ever-dependable followers. However, most influencers are keen on working only with businesses that align with their primary interests and won't be willing to promote any products that their followers will dislike or find useless.

2. **Shaping perceptions:** With positive content that can shift their audience's perceptions about a brand or product, influencers wield a huge influence on their followers' reactions to businesses and their products. Influencers' audience can be urged to consider a brand favorably, and this can cause them to positively associate with those businesses and purchase their products/services, resulting in strong brand affinity or loyalty.

3. **Establishing credibility:** By demonstrating their admirable experience, expertise, and authority on some important concepts to their audience, influencers build credibility and trust over time. So, when they recommend a brand or a product, their followers will genuinely respond to that recommendation, believing that the influencers have deep knowledge in that area. The loyal influencers' audience does not necessarily perceive products or brands mentioned by their influencers in the same light as traditional advertising; so, the brand being promoted by influencers can be recognized as credible and worth patronizing.

4. **Driving engagement and conversion:** With their detailed and incredible product reviews, sponsored content, or tutorials, influencers can tremendously encourage engagement and conversions on businesses' websites. By reading about the great features of a product and the apparent benefits they can derive from using it, the influencers' audience will be motivated to make a purchase or take action on the business' website.

5. **Enhancing brand image:** When brands collaborate with the right influencers that embody their values, aesthetics, and personalities, they can maintain or improve their impressive brand image in the marketplace. Moreover, they can enhance their brand equity and expand their market share. Consumers are mostly interested in buying from brands that have a good image or reputation.

It is clear from all indications that businesses can gain a lot from partnering with influencers to help them broaden their brand awareness, increase brand equity, and draw new consumers to their products/services while leveraging their credibility and trust. The most effective collaboration with influencers occurs when their values, personalities, and interests match with those of the brands they are promoting, and their audience's expectations are met.

In order to fully understand how influencers can play a significant role in transforming a brand's image, it is quite helpful to describe, in detail, what a brand image system is. In principle, a brand image system is a collection of unique characteristics, associations, and elements that vividly portray the brand and indicate how consumers perceive it. It consists of both tangible and intangible aspects that consistently influence how consumers feel about a brand, which intrinsically affects their interaction with it.

1. **Brand identity:** This refers to the visual and verbal components that represent a particular brand, and they may include imagery, colors, typography, logo, and messaging. With its unique brand identity, a business can easily differentiate itself from its competitors, and consumers will be able to easily identify it and/or its products.

2. **Brand personality:** A brand's personality is the human-like attributes that consumers associate with it. It is not rare to hear people refer to a brand as being friendly, reliable, innovative, or adventurous. These brand characteristics encourage consumers to form an emotional bond with some businesses, especially if they seem caring and dependable.

Through its personality, consumers can detect a brand's voice, values, and culture.

3. **Brand values:** Consumers are attracted to brands because of their inherent values. By definition, a brand's value comprises its principles, beliefs, and ideals as indicated in its mission/vision statements. Today, consumers are quite excited to relate with brands that demonstrate a high degree of social responsibility, ethics, integrity, and authenticity. By extension, brands that are eco-friendly can easily draw health-conscious consumers to themselves; the same thing applies to other brands promoting other social causes that people really care about.

4. **Brand associations:** Nowadays, consumers may decide to form clubs or associations around brands that they are passionate about. This mental bonding, or strong loyalty, helps consumers deepen their experiences, perceptions, and interactions with the brands. Some of the benefits of participating in brand associations may include but are not limited to receiving members-only discounts, sharing memorable events with other association members, and receiving member-specific customer service. Most brands appreciate positive associations from their customers because this helps in boosting their image to a great extent.

5. **Brand reputation:** A brand's reputation is directly linked to its past, glowing performance, reputation, and actions in the marketplace, and consumers are quick to identify which brands have a great, admirable reputation or not. Consumers will be reluctant to purchase from or interact with any brand that lacks a good reputation as shown in its lack of credibility, reliability, trust, ethics, and goodwill.

6. **Brand experience:** Brand experience refers to the sum total of interactions and connections consumers have with a brand which inspire them to keep purchasing things from the brand. A positive brand experience, from a consumer's perspective, can mean a smooth consumer experience

obtainable from great customer service, satisfactory product offerings, proper marketing communications, and comfortable brand environments. Consumers naturally develop favorable and positive feelings toward great brand experiences.

7. **Brand communication:** These include brand messaging, narratives, and stories that brands communicate to their existing and prospective customers, possibly through a multichannel approach. The brand communication that is considered effective must align with the brand's overall values, personality, and identity, and it must be consistent and coherent so that consumers can easily identify it. Businesses should avoid releasing misleading information and falsehoods that can put their brand image in danger.

In summary, a well-managed brand image system, comprising the brand elements already explained in this section, can help a brand maintain its great image, boost consumer loyalty, and accomplish outstanding success in the marketplace.

Some powerful influencers, who are also world-famous celebrities, are brands themselves—they perpetually work on protecting their credibility and brand images. People like Christiano Ronaldo, Taylor Swift, Lionel Messi, Jeniffer Lopez, etc. are known for brand endorsements. Big brands that can afford to pay huge amounts of money for endorsements do go into partnerships with these celebrity brands. Some examples of these successful partnerships include the collaboration between Selene Gomez and Pantene; Christiano Ronaldo and Herbalife; and Messi and Pepsi.

11.9 Measuring The Success of a Marketing Campaign

It is imperative for businesses to measure the success of their campaigns, and highlighted below are some of the most important key performance indicators (KPIs) that can be used for this purpose. However, it is of paramount importance that the KPIs should align with campaign objectives.

1. **Return on Investment (ROI):** The ROI helps estimate the effectiveness and profitability of the campaign. It is usually calculated by deducting the expenses/investments on campaigns from the total revenue accrued (including cost savings) as a result of the marketing campaign.

2. **Sales metrics:** One of the ways businesses can identify the impact of their marketing campaigns on conversions, revenue, and sales is to utilize sales metrics. This analytic tool measures the actual number of units of a product sold and their average order value during the campaign.

3. **Conversion rate:** This metric reveals the number of users who took certain actions owing to the marketing campaign. They may make a purchase, fill out a form, or sign up for a newsletter.

4. **Website traffic and engagement:** The user engagement and events on a website can be measured using this KPI, which tracks the website traffic, revealing the number of visitors, time spent on each page, bounce rate, and page views.

5. **Brand awareness and reach:** To measure how marketing campaigns are contributing to brand visibility and awareness, it is important to measure activities like brand mentions, new visitors to the website, search volume, and social media impressions.

6. **Customer Acquisition Cost (CAC):** It is important for businesses to know how many new customers they can acquire per marketing spend. The customer acquisition cost metric helps them to do just that, and to discover the effectiveness of their campaigns.

7. **Customer Lifetime Value (CLV):** If many of the customers that are brought to a business through a marketing campaign stay with the brand for a long time, their CLV value will be positive, meaning that their lifetime value (spending on the business' products) justifies the marketing investment incurred.

8. **Engagement metrics:** Businesses can detect consumers' engagements and sentiments towards their brands by measuring their interactions with their social media content. If many consumers click through, like, comment, and share a brand's social media post, that indicates an active interest and interaction with that brand.

9. **Customer feedback and surveys:** One of the approaches for determining consumers' preferences, perceptions, and interests in a brand is to periodically collect and analyze feedback from them. This can be done through interviews, surveys, and customer reviews.

10. **Market share and competitive analysis:** It is advisable that businesses regularly analyze their positions in the market by estimating their market share, monitoring what their competitors are doing and how they are doing them, and ensuring that they are appropriately positioning themselves in the market using industry-wide marketing benchmarks and standards.

A simple but practical measurement of a marketing campaign's performance is to look at the steps one had already taken in setting up past marketing campaigns, reviewing the ads and campaigns that were set up many years before by asking the following thoughtful questions:

1. Is the ad on strategy?

2. Is the story relevant to the product and the target?

3. Is it memorable?

4. Is there a possible negative or downside to the story? Does it hurt anybody's feelings?

5. Does the ad lead to an effective call to action? What do you want the target to do "now"?

This is all very simple and let me elaborate on each point. I usually have my students do the opposite, that is, to look for a real campaign and reverse engineer the brief and the campaign in general. It is very educational.

1. Ad on strategy means that the brief has been strictly followed by the creatives. Read the section on marketing and creative briefs for further explanation.

2. The relevance of the story means we are looking for a "borrowed interest", that is, we are using something unrelated to the product to catch anybody's attention. An example is an ad from Dutch TV where consumers would get into a bank to find that there was a party inside, the name of the bank withheld for obvious reasons.

3. Memorable means that people are going to remember it for some reason. Creativity plays its role here.

4. In the ages of political correctness and social media, we do not want anybody saying that our brand offends anybody or recalls any negative idea. This is also why Johnson's bug killers never show a real cockroach but, as far as I remember, a cartoon bug.

5. We need to sell, right? Is it clear what your target audience needs to do at the end of the commercial? This is known as a "call to action" It need not always be direct, but has to be something efficient.

Businesses will be able to achieve their desired goals/objectives and obtain encouraging outcomes from their marketing efforts if they concurrently track and analyze the above-mentioned metrics. Some of the insights they can derive from the metrics include assessing the efficiency of their existing marketing campaigns, identifying areas that require some improvements, and learning the necessary procedures for optimizing their marketing processes in the future.

Quiz

1. **Marketing communications primarily focus on:**

   a. Internal company communication.

   b. Promoting products or services to target audiences.

   c. Research and development of new products.

   d. Managing production and distribution channels.

2. **Integrated Marketing Communications (IMC) aims to:**

   a. Create separate marketing campaigns for each communication channel.

   b. Unify marketing efforts across different channels for maximum impact.

   c. Focus solely on online marketing strategies.

   d. Reduce marketing communication budget.

3. **The consumer journey is primarily influenced by:**

   a. Marketing communications only.

   b. Product features and price alone.

   c. A combination of factors like needs, wants, emotions, and external influences.

   d. Availability of the product in physical stores.

4. **A creative brief is crucial for:**

   a. Internal team communication only.

   b. Ensuring alignment and clear communication with marketing agencies.

   c. Providing detailed product specifications.

   d. Managing customer service inquiries.

5. **Observational research helps understand consumer behavior by:**

   a. Directly asking consumers about their product knowledge.

   b. Observing how consumers interact with products and store environments.

   c. Analyzing financial reports of competitors.

   d. Evaluating the effectiveness of existing marketing campaigns.

6. **Promotions typically focus on:**

   a. Long-term brand building and emotional connection.

   b. Short-term sales with incentives like discounts and contests.

   c. Educating consumers about the product category.

   d. Delivering a unified brand message across all channels.

7. **Strategic advertising aims to achieve:**

   a. Immediate sales increase through discounts.

   b. Long-term brand building and positive brand associations.

   c. Gathering customer feedback through surveys.

   d. Reducing marketing communication costs.

8. **Which of the following is NOT a typical objective of marketing communications?**

   a. Increasing brand awareness and recognition.

   b. Reducing production costs.

   c. Educating consumers about product features and benefits.

   d. Fostering customer loyalty and repeat purchases.

9. **Marketing communications encompass a vast "arsenal" of tools. What does this imply about the field of marketing communications?**

    a. It is a constantly evolving field that requires a variety of tools and approaches.

    b. There is a single best marketing communication tool for every situation.

    c. Marketing communication efforts should be limited to traditional advertising methods.

    d. It is a simple and straightforward discipline with few complexities.

10. **Besides promoting products or services, what are some other goals of marketing communications mentioned in the passage?**

    a. Scheduling production processes and managing inventory.

    b. Increasing brand awareness, educating consumers, and driving sales.

    c. Conducting market research and competitor analysis.

    d. Negotiating contracts with suppliers and vendors.

Answers	1 – b	2 – b	3 – c	4 – b	5 – b
	6 – b	7 – b	8 – c	9 – a	10 – b

Chapter Summary

◆ Marketing communications tools are important tools businesses utilize to advance their marketing efforts while promoting their products/services, and they include PR, advertising, social media, etc.

◆ It is of paramount importance to clearly define the achievable goals, which can include but are not limited to creating more awareness, encouraging consumer loyalty, driving sales, and educating customers.

◆ It is also imperative to know your audience: One of the great advantages of conducting audience analysis is that it makes it easy for businesses to target specific audiences with effective messaging that will resonate with them.

◆ The most sensible approach to maintaining a uniform, consistent messaging about a brand across multiple marketing channels is to implement Integrated Marketing Communication (IMC). This unifies the voice of the brand.

◆ A consumer's journey involves different stages, starting with awareness to consideration, evaluation, purchase, and post-purchase interactions.

◆ Having a deep knowledge of Customer Lifetime Value (CLV) can help businesses understand some of the factors influencing consumer decision-making. These factors include brand loyalty, product complexity, and the perceived risk associated with the product.

◆ To achieve measurable marketing success, it is advisable to have a creative brief in hand; it is simply the roadmap that helps all the teams and agencies working on a marketing effort to know their assigned roles/tasks in order to create an impactful marketing campaign.

◆ Some practical steps businesses can take to fully understand consumers' product knowledge include giving them surveys, asking them to participate in focus groups, conducting observational research, and interacting with consumers on digital platforms (like social media).

◆ Being creative with the marketing content used across different Integrated Marketing Communications (IMC) can significantly increase a business's marketing success rate.

◆ The striking difference between promotions and advertising is that the former offers short-term discounts and price-reduction incentives to consumers while the latter focuses on long-term brand awareness and development.

Chapter 12

Global Consumers: A Myriad of Targets - Ethics in Global Marketing

Chapter twelve considers the complexity of global consumerism by focusing on factors influencing global consumers' behaviors and international marketing, such as cross-cultural communication, ethical issues, and customer segmentation. It investigates how brands proactively manage cross-cultural expectations, meet regulatory requirements, and win consumers' loyalty or trust in the face of mounting challenges relating to privacy and invasive technologies.

Key learning objectives should include the reader's understanding of the following:

- Understanding global consumers and customer behavior
- Segmentation and targeting in global markets
- Ethical considerations in global marketing
- Consumer protection and regulatory compliance
- Future trends and challenges in global marketing ethics

12.1 Understanding Global Consumers and Customer Behavior

It is natural for businesses to plan expansion into international markets as they grow, but this corporate goal or ambition comes with a lot of challenges. It is imperative for such businesses to navigate the complex terrain of global consumerism, which requires understanding global consumers, their behaviors, cultural orientations, personal preferences, and purchasing patterns. Any business aspiring to go international must adapt its marketing initiatives so as to effectively and successfully engage with diverse global audiences.

Largely influenced by their different cultures, social norms, technological advancements, and economic conditions, global consumers display different behaviors that are characteristic of their segments or demographics. However, through comprehensive market research, businesses can obtain useful information regarding the behaviors, preferences, needs, and expectations of their targeted global audiences.

It is equally important to respect global ethics when it comes to marketing to global audiences. It is expedient that businesses cautiously manage the issues of cultural sensitivities, operational ethics, and legal regulations to ensure that their marketing efforts are globally acceptable, recognized, and effective. Some attributes of ethical marketing include but are not limited to trust building, enduring relationships with customers, long-term credibility, and sustainable business growth.

12.2 Segmentation and Targeting in Global Markets

Despite the high level of interconnection among people across the globe, businesses still need to segment and target specific global consumers so as to make a success of their plans to expand into international markets. Having a profound understanding of consumer segmenting and targeting can help businesses to be quite aware of and respect different cultures, norms, and expectations in order to win global consumers' trust and loyalty and serve them well.

The number of available segments multiplies tenfold, or even more, when you analyze alternatives in international markets. Take for instance a brand like Doritos. They reportedly have close to 200 flavors internationally.[13] Or brands like Fanta, which is more popular in countries like India or Mexico than it is in the US. There are approximately 200 different flavors of this drink.[14] Now, let us imagine segments if you combine flavors, bottle size, cans vs bottles, dispensers, prices, marketing channels, and local promotions, among the many variables designed to fit into one specific segment for each region and country where these brands are operated. This is the real complexity of international marketing when these brands sometimes have sales that are larger than the economies of medium-sized countries! By the way, that is exactly what Dorito's brand manager said to the audience to a surprised group of MBA students, including myself.

The chapter on segmentation and targeting deserves a closer look from an international marketing perspective. When I wrote about segmentation, I said that it should be Demographic, Behavioral, Attitudinal, and Aspirational, if you have more than one market, then you are multiplying segmentation options. It is totally false that international marketing can be done just by selecting the same market and applying it to a new country. This never, ever happens. Your marketing channels, your price, and your marketing media will be different. Do I need to continue? So, research here is mandatory.

---

13 https://www.taquitos.net/snack_guide/Doritos#:~:text=Doritos%3A,198%20flavors

14 https://nowthatsnifty.blogspot.com/2018/07/list-of-all-fanta-flavors-from-around.html

12.3 Ethical Considerations in Global Marketing

Businesses engaging in global marketing are expected to be ethical in all their approaches. Here are some essential factors that must be put into consideration while marketing to consumers that cut across different regions, demographics, and cultures:

1. **Cultural sensitivity:** It is advisable for businesses marketing to global consumers to pay serious attention to the striking cultural differences among people; what may be tenable in one culture may be sadly considered a show of utter contempt or disrespect in another. To prevent an instance of unintentionally promoting a negative image or stereotype associated with certain demographics, it is important for businesses to conduct in-depth research about their target global audience and approach them in a way that is culturally acceptable to them.

2. **Environmental impact:** Environmentally friendly businesses with great sustainability initiatives in their global marketing are mainly trusted by their global audience. Therefore, it is imperative for businesses to incorporate practices that will reduce operational wastes, and carbon footprint, and encourage environmental conservation activities. It is inappropriate for businesses to engage in greenwashing—the dubious practice of making a product, policy, or activity appear environmentally friendly when in actual fact it is not.

3. **Fair labor practices:** Embracing ethics in their global marketing entails that businesses will engage in fair labor practices such as ensuring that the human rights of all its supply chain workers are respected. This further requires that they are paid fairly, given excellent working conditions, and unexposed to exploitative labor practices like the hiring of child labor.

4. **Transparency and honesty:** It is advisable for businesses to engage global consumers truthfully and transparently because making deceptive claims in communications and marketing messaging will only cause them to distrust the brand. Misleading advertisements, false claims about a product's features or capabilities, and fraudulent pricing strategies can significantly hurt any brand's reputation.

5. **Respect for local laws and regulations:** There are usually local laws and regulations that global marketers are expected to respect and abide by. These may include laws regulating advertising, consumers' privacy, product labeling, product pricing, and other essential aspects of marketing. Failure to abide by these local laws and regulations may result in a hefty fine, legal suit, and public disgrace or defamation.

6. **Social responsibility:** The primary reason businesses set up their corporate social responsibility (CSR) initiatives is to be able to contribute meaningfully and positively to the regions where they are based or operating from. This involves starting or promoting community development projects, charitable causes, and sustainable or environmentally friendly activities. Well-implemented CSR programs can build a strong bridge between businesses and their host communities.

Businesses can successfully win the trust of global consumers, create an impressive brand image, and become part of a thriving group of organizations that operate ethically and sustainably if all the above-mentioned steps are taken into consideration and properly implemented.

Looking at this important issue from another standpoint, let's consider the case of Dolce & Gabbana. Chinese stores dropped products from their lines, following racist allegations.[15] What brand manager in his/her right mind would want such an

---

15 https://www.theguardian.com/world/2018/nov/23/dolce-gabbana-vanishes-from-chinese-retail-sites-amid-racist-ad-backlash

outcome? Who wants to lose money out of insensitivity? I am sure that nobody.

Being a responsible brand is a matter of being good citizens of this planet. This is critical. Additionally, it is a sound business practice. Period.

12.4 Consumer Protection and Regulatory Compliance

The following reasons explain why consumer protection and regulatory compliance are two main requirements for any business that wants to operate internationally:

1. **Legal compliance:** It is very important for businesses to comply with the local laws and regulations in each locality where they are operating. This may require that they wholly abide by the local labor laws, advertising regulations, consumer protection laws, product safety laws, data protection and privacy laws, and other mandatory legal requirements.

2. **Consumer rights:** Consumer rights, supported by laws in many countries, aim to protect consumers from businesses' sharp and deceptive practices, such as selling inferior products, discriminatory pricing, misleading advertisements, etc. Any business that aspires to serve global consumers must understand the scope of consumer rights laws in each of its targeted countries, protecting their privacy and rights to seek amends for any mistreatment.

3. **Product safety:** It is part of global consumer rights that they are offered safe products and services that will not harm or hurt them in any way. It is expedient for businesses operating internationally to comply with all the required local product safety requirements, which may include

adhering to product safety standards, proper product labeling, and certifications.

4. **Transparency and disclosure:** Companies should be transparent in all their communications with consumers so as to gain their trust. This means that they should be clear and precise in transmitting information about their products and services, terms and conditions, pricing, return policies, and warranties to consumers so that they can use that accurate information to make informed purchasing decisions.

5. **Data privacy and security:** As significant aspects of business activities are already online and fully digitized, companies need to be proactive in handling their customers' private information. One approach to safeguarding consumers' private data and security is to abide by all data protection laws, like the EU's General Data Protection Regulation (GDPR). It is equally essential that businesses put in place some security systems that will prevent hackers or unauthorized persons from accessing and misusing consumers' sensitive data.

6. **Ethical business practices:** Companies are expected by laws to operate in an ethical manner by protecting consumer rights and embracing global standards in advertising, marketing, and customer service. Therefore, it is imperative for businesses to shun any practices that could be considered manipulative or deceptive; they should rather give consumers the power to independently make their informed decisions.

7. **Consumer redressal mechanisms:** As part of their superb customer service, businesses should create an effective avenue for disgruntled customers to complain about any products/services they are dissatisfied with so that their issues can be timely resolved in a transparent manner. This requires setting up an in-house department for hearing consumers' grievances and/or making an alternative

provision for dispute resolution by an external tribunal or consumer protection Ombudsman.

8. **Corporate Social Responsibility (CSR):** By truly implementing CSR policies, such as supporting philanthropic efforts, promoting environmentally friendly activities, and protecting the vulnerable members of society, businesses can demonstrate their strong commitment to people and community development. Well-implemented CSR programs can earn a company a good reputation and enduring loyalty.

Companies can maintain robust and mutually beneficial relationships with their customers around the world if they pay serious attention to consumer protection, focus on operating legally and ethically, and serve their customers with good intentions all the time. In return, they will gain their customers' loyalty, trust, and patronage and be able to stay out of legal and ethical problems.

There are obviously, important differences in quality standards for global markets even within the same brands. Take the case of Australia and the car industry[16]. Given that this government is late in signing international pollution standards, automakers have a lower-cost competitive landscape and have no option but to sell more polluting cars. This is where governments become fundamental parts of competitive markets.

---

16 https://www.abc.net.au/news/2021-10-14/australia-dumping-ground-for-polluting-cars-euro-6-standards/100535418

Quiz

1. **Consumers across the globe exhibit a variety of:**

   a. Hair colors

   b. Cultural backgrounds and purchasing habits

   c. Favorite sports teams

   d. Preferred vacation destinations

2. **Understanding the impact of _____ is crucial when targeting consumers in different regions.**

   a. Only economic conditions

   b. Cultural norms, economic conditions, technological advancements, AND social trends

   c. Just technological advancements

   d. Only government regulations

3. **Cultural sensitivity in marketing is important to avoid:**

   a. Highlighting product features

   b. Misinterpretations or stereotypes

   c. Using bright colors

   d. Focusing on price comparisons

4. **Ethical marketing practices include:**

   a. Exaggerated claims about product benefits

   b. Transparency and honesty in communication

   c. Ignoring environmental concerns

   d. Targeting vulnerable populations with manipulative tactics

5. **Businesses need to adapt their marketing strategies to effectively connect with:**

    a. Only high-income consumers

    b. All consumers, regardless of location

    c. Consumers who speak the same language

    d. Only online shoppers

6. **Aligning with local laws and regulations helps businesses avoid:**

    a. Higher marketing costs

    b. Legal and reputational risks

    c. Needing to translate product labels

    d. Experiencing cultural misunderstandings

7. **Businesses that prioritize both understanding global consumers and ethical marketing practices are positioned for:**

    a. Short-term profit gains

    b. Sustainable growth and success

    c. Ignoring local competition

    d. Reducing product quality standards

8. **The passage emphasizes the importance of:**

    a. Focusing solely on profit margins

    b. Navigating the complexities of international markets

    c. Ignoring cultural differences in marketing

    d. Prioritizing speed over ethical considerations

9. **The chapter titled "A World of Consumers" suggests that global marketing requires an understanding of what?**

   a. A standardized approach that works universally.

   b. The diverse preferences and cultural backgrounds of consumers worldwide.

   c. Only the economic conditions of major developed countries.

   d. A focus on technological advancements for online marketing.

10. **Why is it important to understand factors like "cultural norms, economic conditions, technological advancements, and social trends" when targeting global consumers?**

    a. These factors have no significant impact on consumer behavior.

    b. Understanding these factors allows businesses to tailor marketing strategies for different regions.

    c. These factors are only relevant for marketing complex technical products.

    d. Businesses should focus solely on product features and price when marketing globally.

Answers	1 – b	2 – b	3 – b	4 – b	5 – b
	6 – b	7 – b	8 – b	9 – b	10 – b

Chapter Summary

◆ Global consumers have varied preferences, cultural backgrounds, and purchasing habits.

◆ Factors like cultural norms, economic conditions, technological advancements, and social trends all influence consumer behavior across the globe.

◆ Thorough market research and consumer analysis are essential for understanding target audiences in different regions and cultures.

◆ Cultural sensitivity, environmental responsibility, fair labor practices, transparency, and compliance with local laws are all crucial ethical considerations in global marketing.

◆ By integrating ethical considerations into marketing practices, businesses build trust and credibility with consumers worldwide.

◆ Successful global marketing requires adapting strategies to resonate with diverse global audiences effectively.

◆ Aligning with local laws and regulations mitigates legal and reputational risks when entering new markets.

◆ Embracing corporate social responsibility creates long-term value for both the company and society, fostering sustainable global growth.